God at Every Gate

BRENDAN O'MALLEY is a parish priest, College Chaplain and Officer for Pastoral Care and Counselling in the Diocese of St David's, Wales. He is of Irish descent, Scottish birth, Welsh adoption and a former Cistercian monk. His interests lie particularly in pilgrimage and in monastic and Celtic spirituality. His previous publications include the award-winning *The Animals of St Gregory* (Paulinus Press, 1981); *A Pilgrim's Manual, St David's* (Paulinus Press, 1985); *A Welsh Pilgrim's Manual* (Gomer Press, 1989) and *Celtic Spirituality* (Church in Wales Publications, 1992). He is also author of the forthcoming *Pilgrim Guide to St David's*, to be published by the Canterbury Press Norwich.

D1395800

GOD AT EVERY GATE

Prayers and blessings for pilgrims

BRENDAN O'MALLEY

CANTERBURY
PRESS
Norwich

Unless otherwise mentioned the scripture verses quoted in this publication are from The New English Bible (NEB), The Revised English Bible (REB), The New Jerusalem Bible (NJB), and The New International Version (NIV).

My warmest thanks are due to Beenie Phoenix for drafting the typescript, and Christine Smith, my publisher, for her humour and patience.

Every effort has been made to trace the copyright holders of material quoted in this book. Information on any omissions should be sent to the publishers who will make full acknowledgment in any future editions.

BRENDAN O'MALLEY

© in this compilation Brendan O'Malley 1997
First published 1997 by The Canterbury Press Norwich
(a publishing imprint of Hymns ancient & Modern Limited
a registered charity)
St Mary's Works, St Mary's Plain,
Norwich, Norfolk, NR3 3BH

Brendan O'Malley has asserted his right under the Copyright,
Designs and Patents Act, 1988, to be identified as Author of this Work

British Library Cataloguing in Publication Data

A catalogue record for this book is available from the British Library

ISBN 1–85311–162–7

Typeset by David Gregson Associates, Beccles, Suffolk
Printed and bound in Great Britain by
Athenæum Press Ltd, Gateshead, Tyne & Wear

To my first Pilgrims –
Kate, Charles and Laura

Pilgrim, take care your journey's not in vain,
a hazard without profit, without gain;
the King you seek you'll find in Rome, it's true
but only if he travels on the way with you.
                    Medieval Irish Lyric

Contents

Inscape

Our journey had advanced,
   Our feet were almost come
To that odd fork in Being's road,
   Eternity by term.

Our pace took sudden awe,
   Our feet reluctant led
Before were cities, but between,
   The forest of the dead.

Retreat was out of hope,
   Behind, a sealed route,
Eternity's white flag before,
   And God at every gate.

                    Emily Dickinson

INTRODUCTION

Keep open – Oh, keep open ... my eyes, my
mind, my heart.
Herman Hagedorn

'Our real journey in life is interior,' wrote
Thomas Merton as he prepared to set out on
his last journey to the East, a short time before
his death.

God calls us to seek him at different times in
our lives. He may intimate His presence at a
time of crisis, a time of decision, of suffering,
joy, happiness or despair. He may ask us to
show courage.

> But at once Jesus called out to them saying,
> 'Courage! It is I! Do not be afraid.' It was
> Peter who answered. 'Lord,' he said, 'if it
> is you, tell me to come to you across the
> water.' 'Come,' said Jesus. Then Peter got
> out of the boat and started walking towards
> Jesus across the water, but as soon as he
> felt the force of the wind, he took fright
> and began to sink. 'Lord! save me!' he
> cried. Jesus put out his hand at once and
> held him. 'Man of little faith,' he said,
> 'Why did you doubt?' And as they got into
> the boat the wind dropped. The men in the
> boat bowed down before him and said,
> 'Truly you are the Son of God.'
> *Matthew 14: 27–33* J.B.

1

We are all at some time or another in our lives asked to 'walk on water', to trust God and set out in faith at His command over the troubled waters of our lives. The solid ground that previously seemed to be so certain, secure and inviolate can vanish from beneath our feet. All may appear to be sinking. We may be going through a period of doubt and uncertainty concerning our faith, our future or a relationship.

Whatever the circumstance, it is often then that we hear the call of God and the invitation to rely on the word of Christ. This Word often speaks to us secretly in the silence of our hearts. God calls us through the elemental and the transcendental, to the truth which is both deep within us and beyond us.

Any journey He calls us to make is a foretaste of our final journey across the waters of death. One day He will call us to leave the earthly 'boat' on which we have been carried across the stormy waters of this world. He will beckon us to reach out and be held by Him, safe and secure, in a peace which will set our troubled hearts at rest.

God in Christ is calling us today to reactivate the will to desire, know and love Him. It is the one thing that matters. To know and love Him effectively we need to learn to know and love ourselves for what we are: unique creations, infinitely lovable, created in the image and likeness of God. In seeking God down the pathways of our lives we cannot afford to pass ourselves by. To do so would be to evade Him . . .

People travel to wonder
at the height of the mountains,
at the huge waves of the sea,
at the long courses of rivers,
at the vast compass of the ocean,
at the circular motion of the stars,
and they pass themselves by without
    wondering.

St Augustine

Jesus Christ came into our world as Light shining in darkness. The darkness did not understand the Light and sought to extinguish it. The work of the Risen Christ is to fulfil the prophecies of old that God would lead His people in pilgrimage to the Promised Land. He would lead them from darkness into light. Christ is the Light of the world and we Christians have been called to see His light shining out 'like shook foil' in all created being ...

The world is charged with the grandeur of
    God
It will flame out, like shining from shook
    foil ...

Gerard Manley Hopkins

Christ is still present in and on this earth and in all whom we meet. The love and power of God is speaking to us through all of Creation. This Word is spoken in the grass, the animals, the rocks, the trees, the sun, moon, stars, oceans ...

As the rain and snow come down from the
    heavens

and do not return there without watering
   the earth,
making it produce grain
to give seed for sowing and bread to eat,
so is it with my word issuing from my
   mouth;
it will not return to me empty
without accomplishing my purpose
and succeeding in the task for which I sent
   it.

Isaiah 55: 10, 11 R.E.B.

Are we sensitive to this Word, the grandeur of
God? Where have we been whilst the creative
power of God has been tumbling forth, reaching
out to us in the myriad circumstances of our
lives? Have we been asleep?
   What has happened to our world?

Its watchmen are all blind,
they know nothing.
Dumb watchdogs all, unable to bark,
they dream, lie down, and love to sleep.
Greedy dogs, never satisfied . . .
Who understand nothing.

Isaiah 56:10 N.J.B.

We see and yet we do not see. We admire the
clouds, the trees and yet fail to see the beauty
of God shining through them. So much of God's
loving presence invades us, at each moment,
and yet we fail to respond. God's energizing
love is in each event, each moment of our lives.
Most of us are asleep to that presence. Jesus
Christ is called to us: 'Why are you sleeping?'
(*Luke 22:46*) 'Wake up! Follow me!'

4

The modern illness of stress and fatigue, boredom and the constant search for false happiness, temporarily assuaged by consumerism, seeks healing. There is a thirst for the mystical, the spiritual. Nowadays it would seem there is great interest in prayer and meditation. People are making voyages to faraway places to venerate the physical reminders of holy people. It is because these holy places are soaked with Presence; they are nature adorned by grace, energized by the act of prayer and hallowed by the presence of those who were themselves fulfilled temples of Holy Spirit, those who contemplated, 'con-templed', God.

In ancient times pilgrims travelled with the intention of remaining at their holy destination, never to return home. They argued that to be buried in a holy place gave one a greater chance of rising heavenwards on the Last Day.

Today there is a resurgence in the desire to 'make pilgrimage'. The difference between a tourist and a pilgrim is that a pilgrim seeks an experience of God. What is also appealing to many people is that modern pilgrimage is not a stereotyped form of religious practice. It is personal. And yet each of us is part of the larger network of light, one of many pilgrims throughout the world travelling from point to point, seeking the nectar of spiritual and physical enlightment at a holy place and depositing the pollen of our own spiritual energy in the form of grace received through the practice of prayer. We are spiritual bees in search of the hidden word ...

more desirable than gold,
even than the finest gold;
his word, sweeter than honey,
that drips from the comb.

Psalm 19:10 N.J.B.

The modern person tends to reject 'religion' whilst at the same time opting for 'spirituality'. Possibly it is received opinion of the Church as 'institution' that they are discarding. Perhaps 'religion' is synonymous with 'authority'. The sad effect of this attitude is that ritual as a vehicle of spirit is neglected. We thereby lose the means of contacting that which is deep within us, whom we know as God.

Spirituality needs shape, needs structure, a channel or track to run along in order to get anywhere. Religion is the way and the means by which we link the 'earthly' to the 'heavenly'. Just as spirituality needs religion the pilgrim needs the guidance of the Church in order to arrive safely and in good order. Without the Church, with all its human frailty, we tend to follow our own whims and fancies and become dispersed, lost in a desert of selfishness. Inspired by Christ's teaching, who bade the Church teach all nations, we are able to move forward nourished by right teaching (doctrine), word and sacrament. A day's food for a day's journey. Therefore to go on pilgrimage is not simply to journey to a holy place. There is the inner journey as well as the outer journey. To enable the inner journey to take place we need to *practise* the presence of God. The physical place is important, and so is the physical act. A sacrament is a sign that signifies and gives life.

6

It effects what it symbolizes. Pilgrimage is, if you like, a sacrament-on-foot! The physical journey will effect a change in us. We need, however, to become spiritually aware, looking inwardly over the interior landscape upon which we make our sacred journey, travelling in the company of the People of God, the Angels and the Saints.

It has been said that physically we are recycled stardust; the microcosm of the macrocosm; a tiny planet in miniature journeying over the larger planet within the cosmos. In many ways we are similar to those Russian dolls which fit one within the other.

Christ calls out to us, seeking us through all whom we meet. He would hold us in the hollow of His hand. Pilgrimage is a valid means of making for this truth a symbol which binds and holds the physical and spiritual truth together.

God at Every Gate is by definition a manual, a book at hand to be used as a companion on the journey. It is also a prayer book to be dipped into as an effective means of relating the 'without' to the 'within'. For example, if you rest by the water's edge than look up the section 'Rivers', 'Water', or perhaps 'Ocean Blessing' to find appropriate meditations. Each section consists of a little 'office' of devotion in its own right. If you are 'faint and tempest-beaten', whether in body or spirit, the heading for you may be 'Suffering' or 'Anxiety'. When trees, birds or animals are encountered, or temptation, joy or hope is felt, then look up the contents listing and use the book as a means of raising your heart and mind to God.

7

There is a deeper way of using the meditations in this book. For example, the wilderness can be seen as symbolic of the waste places within each one of us. When in a lonely or desolate place remember that it was the wilderness into which Jesus went to fast and pray. He was tempted in the desert. Our own wild and untamed moods are the waste places, the wilderness, wherein we are tempted. A true office or manual of daily prayer needs to prompt within us the inspiration to pray from the depths of the heart; its very structure is a springboard to contemplation.

Under the general heading in each section will be found 'Focus', which encapsulates the general thought or theme. 'Meditation' follows, to be read quietly or, if possible, spoken aloud. Pray over it as you read it, enunciating the words slowly and thoughtfully. Seize on the sentence or phrase which attracts you most and ask God to reveal its deepest meaning to your heart. Contemplate the mystery of God's revealed word and feed on the spiritual nourishment it offers you.

A Psalm is suggested for further reflection. The Psalms make wonderful companions as we walk along the path of life. They are the perfect prayers for enabling the truth about God and about ourselves to spread through the blood and deepen the traveller's awareness of God.

The Collect 'collects' together the thoughts, emotions and inspiration into one, and the Centring Prayer offers a sentence to be memorized and used as a rhythmic prayer for walking in the footsteps of love.

I implore you, good Jesus, that as in your mercy you have given me to drink in with delight the words of your knowledge, so of your loving kindness you will also grant me one day to come to you, the fountain of all wisdom, and to stand for ever before your face. Amen.

A prayer of the Venerable Bede

PREPARATION

O LORD,
forgive what I have been,
sanctify what I am,
and order what
I shall be

ANONYMOUS

Confession and Forgiveness

FOCUS

And when they reached the place called The
Skull, they crucified him there ... Jesus said,
'Father, forgive them; they do not know what
they are doing.'   *Luke 23:33–34* R.E.B.

MEDITATION

Have mercy on me, God, in your
    kindness.
In your compassion blot out my offence.
O wash me more and more from my guilt
and cleanse me from my sin.

My offences truly I know them;
my sin is always before me.
Against you, you alone, have I sinned,
what is evil in your sight I have done.

A pure heart create for me, O God,
put a steadfast spirit within me.
Do not cast me away from your presence,
nor deprive me of your Holy Spirit.

O rescue me, God, my helper,
and my tongue shall sing out your
    goodness.
O Lord, open my lips
and my mouth shall declare your praise.
                Psalm 51:1–4, 10, 11, 14, 15[1]

Now my heart submits to you, imploring
    your great goodness.
I have sinned, Lord, I have sinned,
and I acknowledge my transgressions.
I beg and beseech you,

spare me, Lord, spare me;
destroy me not with my transgressions on
    my head,
do not be angry with me for ever,
or store up punishment for me.
Do not condemn me to the depths of the
    earth,
for you, Lord, are the God of the
    penitent.
You will show your goodness towards
    me,
for, unworthy as I am, you will save me
    in your great mercy;
and I shall praise you continually all the
    days of my life.
The whole host of heaven sings your
    praise,
and yours is the glory for ever. Amen.

from The Prayer of Manasseh (Apocrypha) N.E.B.

COLLECT

> O Lord,
> forgive what I have been,
> sanctify what I am,
> and order what I shall be.
> *Anon.*

May almighty God bless us, keep us from
    all evil and lead us to everlasting life.
    Amen.

CENTRING PRAYER

> Lord Jesus Christ, Son of God,
> have mercy on me, a sinner.

Renewal of Baptismal Promises

Blessed are those who observe the instructions of the Lord, who seek him with all their hearts, and doing no evil, who walk in his ways.

Psalm 119:2

A Baptismal Creed

I believe and trust in God the Father who
    created all that is.
I believe and trust in His Son Jesus
    Christ who redeemed mankind.
I believe and trust in His Holy Spirit who
    gives life to the people of God.
I believe and trust in one God:
Father, Son and Holy Spirit. Amen.[2]

Blessed are you, Lord God, Our Father.
You deliver us from every evil,
You grant us peace in our day and
    protect us from all anxiety.
I proclaim Jesus Christ the way to the
    Father.
May He bless me on my journey and
    bring me in union with Him in Heaven.
May the same Jesus Christ nourish me in
    His truth and inspire me to persevere
    to the end.

May the life of Christ within me from
    Baptism sustain and deepen my love of
    the Father.

And, the blessing of Almighty God, the
    Father, the Son and the Holy Spirit,
    come down upon me and remain with
    me for ever and ever. Amen.[3]

Blessing at the Beginning of a Pilgrimage

Guide me in your truth and teach me, Lord, for you are the God who saves me. *Psalm 25:5*

O thou full of compassion,
I commit and commend myself unto thee,
    in whom I am,
    and live,
    and know.

Be thou the goal of my pilgrimage,
    and my rest by the way.

Let my soul take refuge
    from the crowding turmoil
    of worldly thoughts
    beneath the shadow of thy wings;
let my heart, this sea of restless waves,
    find peace in thee, O God.

Thou bounteous giver of all good gifts,
    give to him who is weary refreshing food,
gather our distracted thoughts and powers
    into harmony again;
    and set the prisoner free.

See, he stands at thy door and knocks;
    be it opened to him,
    that he may enter with a free step,
    and be quickened by thee.

For thou art the well-spring of life,
    the light of eternal brightness,
    wherein the just live
    who love thee.

Be it unto me according to thy word.

St Augustine

Heavenly Father, protector of all who trust in you, you led your people in safety through the desert and brought them to a land of plenty. Guide me as I begin my journey today. Fill me with your spirit of love. Preserve me from all harm and bring me safely to my destination.

I ask this through Christ our Lord.[4]

or

Father, you have called us to a pilgrimage of faith. The light of your truth summons us, and the call of faith is a constant challenge on our journey. We give thanks for the desire to seek you: we give thanks for voices from the past that offer guidance, for signposts pointing to the next stage, for companions who share the journey, for footsteps in the sand of pilgrims before us, for the conviction that, unseen but not unknown, you are with us. Father, keep us faithful to the vision, and steadfast on our pilgrimage so that the distant goal may become a reality, and faith at last lead to sight.

Resolutions

Grant me, I beseech thee, O merciful God, prudently to study, rightly to understand, and perfectly to fulfil that which is pleasing to Thee, to the praise and glory of Thy name. Amen.

St Thomas Aquinas

MEDITATION

> Give me my scallop-shell of quiet,
> My staff of faith to walk upon,
> My scrip of joy, immortal diet,
> My bottle of salvation,
> My gown of glory, hope's true gage;
> And thus I'll take my pilgrimage.
>
> Blood must be my body's balmer;
> No other balm will there be given;
> Whilst my soul, like quiet palmer,
> Travelleth towards the land of heaven;
> Over the silver mountains,
> Where spring the nectar fountains;
>   There will I kiss
>   The bowl of bliss;
> And drink mine everlasting fill
> Upon every milken hill.
> My soul will be a-dry before;
> But, after, it will thirst no more.
>
> And by the happy blissful way
> More peaceful pilgrims I shall see,
> That have cast off their rags of clay.
> And walk apparell'd fresh like me.
>   I'll take them first

18

To quench their thirst
And taste of nectar suckets,
At those clear wells
Where sweetness dwells,
Drawn up by saints in crystal buckets.
Sir Walter Raleigh

Read Psalm 31

COLLECT

To thee, O Jesu, I direct my eyes;
to thee my hands, to thee my humble
knees;
to thee my heart shall offer sacrifice;
to thee my thoughts, who my thoughts
only sees;
to thee my self – my self and all I give;
to thee I die, to thee I only live.
Sir Walter Raleigh[5]

CENTRING PRAYER

How should I seek you, O Lord?
In seeking you, my God,
I am looking for life's true happiness.
I will seek you so that my soul might live,
since it is you who give the soul its life.
St Augustine Confessions *X, 20*

Promises

> The woods are lovely, dark, and deep,
> But I have promises to keep,
> And miles to go before I sleep,
> And miles to go before I sleep.
>
> *Robert Frost*[6]

MEDITATION

I am praying and appealing to God,
The Son of Mary and the Spirit of truth,
To aid me in distress of sea and of land:
May the Three succour me, may the
    Three shield me,
        May the Three watch me by day and
        by night.

God and Jesus and the Spirit of cleansing
Be shielding me, be possessing me, be
    aiding me,
Be clearing my path and going before my
    soul
In hollow, on hill, on plain.
        On sea and land be the Three aiding
        me.

God and Jesus and the Holy Spirit
Be shielding and saving me,
As Three and as One,
By my knee, by my back, by my side,
        Each step of the stormy world.

Carmina Gadelica III 173[7]

Read Psalm 16

COLLECT

O Lord, be with me at every change and turn of my way as I seek you down the pathway of my life. Help me to keep the promises I have made, through Jesus Christ our Lord. Amen.

CENTRING PRAYER

> O God come to my aid,
> O Lord make haste to help me.

Aspirations

HAPPY *are those whose refuge is in you, whose hearts are set on the pilgrim ways* PSALM 84·5

MEDITATION

Pilgrim, faint and tempest-beaten,
Lift thy gaze, behold and know
Christ the Lamb, our Mediator,
Robed in vestments trailing low;
Faithfulness his golden girdle;
Bells upon his garments ring
Free salvation for the sinner
Through his priceless offering.

Think on this when to your ankles
Scarce the healing waters rise –
Numberless shall be the cubits
Measured to you in the skies.
Children of the resurrection,
They alone can venture here;
Yet they find no shore, no bottom
To Bethesda's waters clear.

O the deeps of our salvation!
Mystery of godliness!
He, the God of gods, appearing
In our fleshly human dress:
He it is who bore God's anger,
In our place atonement made,
Until Justice cried 'Release him,
Now the debt is fully paid'.

22

Blessed hour of rest eternal,
Home at last, all labours o'er;
Sea of wonders never sounded,
Sea where none can find a shore;
Access free to dwell for ever
Yonder with the One in Three;
Deeps no foot of man can traverse –
God and Man in Unity.

Ann Griffiths[8]

Read Psalm 5

COLLECT

My God, my love: thou art all mine, and I am all
thine. Enlarge me in love; that with the inner
mouth of my heart I may taste how sweet it is
to love. Let me love thee more than myself, and
myself only for thee, and in thee all that love
thee truly; as the law of love commandeth shining forth from thee.   *Thomas à Kempis (1380–1471)*

CENTRING PRAYER

> FATHER,
> I am seeking:
> I am hesitant and uncertain,
> but will you, O God,
> watch over each step of mine
> and guide me.

ST. AUGUSTINE

Hope

Let thy steadfast love, O Lord, be upon us, even
as we hope in thee.   *Psalm 33:22*

MEDITATION

No temptation has seized you except what is
common to man. And God is faithful; he will
not let you be tempted beyond what you can
bear. But when you are tempted, he will also
provide a way out so that you can stand up
under it.   *1 Corinthians 10:13* N.I.V.

Read Psalm 46

COLLECT

O Father, give the spirit power to climb
To the fountain of all light, and be
    purified.
Break through the mists of earth, the
    weight of the clod,
Shine forth in splendour, thou that art
    calm weather,
And quiet resting place for faithful souls.
To see thee is the end and the beginning,
Thou carriest us, and thou dost go
    before,
Thou are the journey, and the journey's
    end.
                                        Boethius

CENTRING PRAYER

> Faith urges us towards you,
> hope guides us
> and love units us to you.
> > *St Augustine*

Trust

There is no place where God is not.
Wherever I go, there God is.
Now and always he upholds me with his power,
and keeps me safe in his love.

Alone with none but thee, my God,
I journey on my way:
What need I fear when thou art near,
O King of night and day?
More safe am I within thy hand
Than if a host should round me stand.

My destined time is known to thee,
And death will keep his hour;
Did warriors strong around me throng,
They could not stay his power:
No wall of stone can man defend
When thou thy messenger dost send.

My life I yield to thy decree,
And bow to thy control
In peaceful calm, for from thine arm
No power can wrest my soul:
Could earthly omens e'er appal
A man that heeds the heavenly call?

The child of God can fear no ill,
His chosen, dread no foe;
We leave our fate with thee, and wait
Thy bidding when to go:
'Tis not from chance our comfort springs,
Thou art our trust, O King of kings.

St Columba

Read Psalm 13

COLLECT

Holy and eternal God, give us such trust in your sure purpose, that we measure our lives not by what we have done or failed to do, but by our faithfulness to you.[9]

CENTRING PRAYER

> I trust in your merciful love,
> Let my heart rejoice in your saving help.
> *Psalm 13:5*

Reconciliation

God ... has entrusted us with the message of
reconciliation.   *2 Corinthians 5:19*

MEDITATION

> Thee, God, I come from, to thee go,
> All day long I like fountain flow
> From thy hand out, swayed about
> Mote-like in thy mighty glow.
>
> What I know of thee I bless,
> As acknowledging thy stress
> On my being and as seeing
> Something of thy holiness.
>
> Once I turned from thee and hid,
> Bound on what thou hadst forbid;
> Sow the wind I would; I sinned:
> I repent of what I did.
>
> Bad I am, but yet thy child.
> Father, be thou reconciled,
> Spare thou me, since I see
> With thy might that thou art mild.
>
> I have life before me still
> And thy purpose to fulfil;
> Yea a debt to pay thee yet:
> Help me, sir, and so I will.
>
> But thou bidst, and just thou art,
> Me shew mercy from my heart
> Towards my brother, every other
> Man my mate and counterpart.
> *Gerard Manley Hopkins*[10]

Read Psalm 32

O Jesus,
Thou brightness of eternal glory,
Thou comfort of the pilgrim soul,
   with thee is my tongue without voice,
   and my very silence speaketh unto thee . . .
Come, O come!
For without thee I shall have no joyful
   day nor hour;
   for thou art my joy,
   and without thee my table is empty . . .
Praise therefore and glory be unto thee,
O Wisdom to the Father;
   let my mouth,
   my soul,
   and all creatures together,
   praise and bless thee.
                                        Thomas à Kempis

CENTRING PRAYER

All shall be well, and all shall be well,
and all manner of thing shall be well.
                                        Julian of Norwich

LANDSCAPE

THERE IS
NO PLACE WHERE
GOD IS NOT;
WHEREVER I GO
THERE
GOD IS

Creation

EARTH is but the frozen echo of the silent voice of God

Man has every right to be anxious about his fate so long as he feels himself to be lost and lonely in the midst of created things. But let him once discover that his fate is bound up with nature itself, and immediately, joyously, he will begin his forward march.   *Pierre Teilhard de Chardin*[11]

MEDITATION

A Song of Creation: Benedicite

1   Bless the Lord all created things:
     sing his praise and exalt him for ever.

2   Bless the Lord you heavens:
     sing his praise and exalt him for ever.

3   Bless the Lord you angels of the Lord:
     bless the Lord all you his hosts:

4   bless the Lord you waters above the
          heavens:
     sing his praise and exalt him for ever.

5   Bless the Lord sun and moon:
     bless the Lord you stars of heaven;

6   bless the Lord rain and dew:
     sing his praise and exalt him for ever.

7   Bless the Lord all winds that blow;
bless the Lord you fire and heat;

8   bless the Lord scorching wind and bitter
cold:
sing his praise and exalt him for ever.

9   Bless the Lord dews and falling snows:
bless the Lord you nights and days;

10   bless the Lord light and darkness:
sing his praise and exalt him for ever.

11   Bless the Lord frost and cold:
bless the Lord you ice and snow;

12   bless the Lord lightnings and clouds:
sing his praise and exalt him for ever.

13   O let the earth bless the Lord:
bless the Lord you mountains and hills;

14   bless the Lord all that grows in the
ground:
sing his praise and exalt him for ever.

15   Bless the Lord you springs:
bless the Lord you seas and rivers;

16   bless the Lord you whales and all that
swim in the waters:
sing his praise and exalt him for ever.

17   Bless the Lord all birds of the air:
bless the Lord you beasts and cattle;

18   bless the Lord all who live on the earth:
sing his praise and exalt him for ever.

19   O people of God bless the Lord:
bless the Lord you priests of the Lord;

20   bless the Lord you servants of the Lord:
     sing his praise and exalt him for ever.

21   Bless the Lord all you of upright spirit:
     bless the lord you that are holy.

22   Bless the Father, the Son and the Holy
         Spirit:
     sing his praise and exalt him for ever.
                    from Song of the Three (Apocrypha)

CENTRING PRAYER

     Help me to hear and understand
     how in the beginning you created
     heaven and earth.
                              St Augustine

EARTH

O let the earth bless the Lord:
bless the Lord you mountains and hills.

Benedicite

MEDITATION

Teach your children
what we have taught our children,
that the earth is our mother.
Whatever befalls the earth
befalls the sons of earth.
If men spit upon the ground,
they spit upon themselves.

This we know.
The earth does not belong to man;
man belongs to earth.
This we know.
All things are connected
like the blood
which unites one family.

All things are connected.
Whatever befalls the earth
befalls the sons of earth.
Man did not weave the web of life,
he is merely a strand in it.
Whatever he does to the web,
he does to himself.

Chief Seattle

Read Psalm 67

COLLECT

Let the heavens and the earth praise Him, the Glorious, and every creature which is in heaven and on earth and under the earth, in the seas and all that are in them.

Let us praise and exalt Him above all forever.

St Francis

CENTRING PRAYER

Bless O God the earth beneath my feet.

Animals

All living beings are bound together by one consciousness.   *Stevie Wonder*

Mole felt a great Awe fall upon him, an awe that
turned his muscles to water, bowed his head,
and rooted his feet to the ground. It was no
panic terror – indeed he felt wonderfully at
peace and happy – but it was an awe that smote
and held him and, without seeing, he knew it
could only mean that some august Presence
was very, very near ... he raised his humble
head; and then, in that utter clearness of the
imminent dawn, while Nature, flushed with fullness of incredible colour, seemed to hold her
breath for the event, he looked in the very eyes
of the Friend and Helper. ...

'Rat!' he found breath to whisper, shaking.
'Are you afraid?'

'Afraid! Of Him? O, never, never! And yet –
and yet – O, Mole, I am afraid!'

Then the two animals, crouching to the earth,
bowed their heads and did worship.
                    Kenneth Grahame, The Wind in the Willows

More things are learnt in the woods than
   from books.
Animals, trees and rocks teach you
   things not to be heard elsewhere.
                                     St Bernard

Praise be thou, O Lord, who hast made every
animal wise in the instinct thou hast given it.

St Adamnan[12]

MEDITATION

The Hermit

I have a bothy in the wood –
none knows it but the Lord, my God;
one wall an ash, the other hazel,
and a great fern makes the door.

The doorsteps are of heather,
the lintel of honeysuckle;
and wild forest all around
drops mast for well-fed swine.

This size my hut: the smallest thing,
homestead amid well-trod paths;
a woman – blackbird clothed and
    coloured –
is singing sweetly from its gable.

*   *   *

Smooth the tresses of yew-green
    yew-trees, glorious potent;
place delicious with great green
    oakwoods increasing blessing.

Tree of apples huge and magic,
    great its graces;
crop in fistfulls from clustered hazel,
    green and branching.

Sparkling wells and water-torrents,
    best for drinking;

green privet there and bird-cherry
  and yew-berries.

Resting there are herded swine,
  goats and piglings;
wild swine too, deer and doe,
  speckled badgers.

Great woodland bands troop like fairies
  to my bothy;
and great delight when timid foxes
  show their faces.

*   *   *

Pigeons cooing, breasts are gleaming,
  beloved flutter;
on my house-top constant music,
  song of thrushes.

Bees and chafers, gentle humming
  and soft crooning;
wild geese come with rough dark music
  before All Hallows.

*   *   *

Then come dear white ones, herons,
  seagulls sea-chant hearing;
no harsh music when grouse is calling
  from russet heather.

I hear the soughing of the pine-trees
  and pay no money;
I am richer far through Christ, my Lord,
  than ever you were.

Though you enjoy all you consume
  and wealth exceeding,
I am grateful for the riches
  my dear Christ brings me.

No hour of trouble like you endure,
　　no din of combat;
I thank the Prince who so endows me
　　in my bothy.

Irish; author unknown (ninth–tenth century)[13]

Read Psalm 148

COLLECT

For those, O Lord, the humble beasts, that bear
with us the burden and heat of the day, and
offer their guileless lives for the well-being of
their countries; we supplicate thy tenderness
of heart, for thou hast promised to save both
man and beast, and great is thy loving kindness,
O Master, Saviour of the world.　　　*Eastern Church*

CENTRING PRAYER

Blessed art thou, O Lord our God, King
　　of the Universe, who hast such as these
　　in thy world.

The Hebrew Prayer Book

Reptiles

Often a man has a fountain of inward liquid but
does not drink from it. It's not that he cannot
understand, it is just that he won't apply himself to the reading of Holy Writ. He knows that
he has the ability to understand by studying,
yet he disdains all study of the lessons of truth.
He knows that the words of Divine utterance
are great, but won't put himself out in order to
understand them. On the other hand, another
man has a thirst for knowledge and doesn't
have the ability; love draws him to meditation,
but his dull sense withstands him and he often
find out, through earnestness of love, that
Divine Law which the cleverer man remains
ignorant of through carelessness. The quick
witted learn nothing of God from disdaining
Him, while the dull follow after Him with
warm affection.   *St Gregory the Great,* Moralia 6, 12

MEDITATION

Brother Lizard was of the slower sort. He had
few apparent gifts; he was not attractive to
look at nor was he clever or quick-witted.
Everything he did was accomplished with
painstaking endeavour. He was the monastery
cook and from his kitchen he poured out his
love in the service of others. He had a happy
heart and his attitude was transmitted in his
work, so that the simple fare he served took on
the element of a sacrament. Through his work,
his love was made visible. In his work, he

found the reality of himself, something no one else could know.

It was sacramental because the more sensitive he was to God in prayer, the more aware he was of the encounter with God in creation. He realized the creative power of God through the work of his hands. Through prayer, he sanctified his work and in this way he himself became a sacrament or gesture of God to his brethren in Christ. Lizard's cooking became part of his ritual, his loving awareness of and reverence for Spirit in matter, and in others. 'Let the brethren serve one another ... for this service brings increase of reward and of charity' (*Rule of St Benedict*).

His loving awareness that all of creation is made sacred by the incarnation of Christ and his reverence for all the materials he handled as signs of God's love, to be used to further that love and so co-create the world in Christ, deepened, the more he encountered Christ in work and prayer.

As any opportunity to give or witness to Love presented itself, Brother Lizard would step forward and serve that need and in so doing would advance slowly towards his Maker. In this way he advanced in the footsteps of Love and the footsteps of God were imprinted upon his heart; they became his way of life. Although he could not see God he tracked Him by His footsteps. This was his prayer, 'I humbly follow after Thee with all my heart and thy right hand is my support' (Psalm 63 : 8).

Brian Brendan O'Malley[14]

Read Psalm 63

Read Psalm 63

COLLECT

> Let nothing disturb thee,
> Nothing affright thee.
> All things are passing,
> God never changeth.
> Patient endurance
> Attaineth to all things.
> Who God possesseth
> In nothing is wanting;
> Alone God sufficeth.
>> *St Teresa of Avila*

CENTRING PRAYER

> Traveller, there is no road,
> the road is made as you go.

I am the Way, the Truth and the Life.   *John 14:6*

Trees

Each bush and oak doth know I AM.
Henry Vaughan

Trees are the earth's endless effort to the listening heaven.
Rabindranath Tagore

MEDITATION

I think that I shall never see
A poem lovely as a tree,
A tree whose hungry mouth is pressed
Against the earth's sweet flowing breast;
A tree that looks at God all day,
And lifts her leafy arms to pray:

A tree that may in summer wear
A nest of robins in her hair;
Upon whose bosom snow has lain;
Who intimately lives with rain.
Poems are made by fools like me,
But only God can make a tree.
Traditional Irish

Read Psalm 74

Thou shalt take to God,
God shall take to thee,
Surrounding thy two feet,
His two hands about thy head.
To thorns of trees or hollies;
A rock thou art at sea.
A fortress thou art on land.
Carmina Gadelica III 197

Almighty one, in the woods I am blessed. Happy everyone in the woods. Every tree speaks through Thee. O God! What glory in the woodland! On the heights is peace – peace to serve Him. *Beethoven*

The tree which moves some to tears of joy is in the eyes of others a green thing which stands in the way. *Blake*

Bless us, Lord Christ, on our pilgrimage, be with us and all who are dear to us, and with everyone we meet. Keep us in the spirit of the Beatitudes: joyful, simple, merciful. Amen.
Brother Roger of Taizé

CENTRING PRAYER

Help me to hear your voice in the trees, O Lord.

Grass

As for us our days are like grass we flower like the flowers of the field, the wind blows and we are gone and our place never sees us again

PSALM 103, 15-16

MEDITATION

I cry
For the lichens and the mosses that grow on
   the stone,
The timeless granite boulders.

I cry
For the grasses and flowers that colour the
Wind-swept landscape.

I cry
For the beauty of the natural world, the perfect
Balance, the perfect poem.

I cry
For all the unborn generations.

47

I cry
For my long lost innocence.

I cry
With my fear.

My tears fall on the stones, the soil,
Make my tears give you life.
Make my despair give you hope.
Make my fear turn to trust.
Make my deeds be enough.

Helen Colebrook[15]

Read Psalm 23

COLLECT

O God we know that all humankind is grass,
which lasts no longer than a flower in the field.
The grass withers, the flower fades, when the
breath of the Lord blows on them.

Your Word endures for ever, enable us to
breathe your Word that we may aspire to heaven through Jesus Christ, Your Son, our Lord.
Amen.

AFTERWORD

All that man has here externally in multiplicity
is intrinsically one. Here all blades of grass,
wood, and stone, all things are one. This is the
deepest depth.   *Meister Eckhart*

CENTRING PRAYER

Come to me, all who labour and are
overburdened, and I will give you rest.
Matthew 11:28 J.B.

Flowers

For see, the winter is past!
The rains are over and gone;
The flowers appear in the countryside;
the season of birdsong is come.

Song of Songs 2:12

MEDITATION

I see his blood upon the rose,
And in the stars the glory of his eyes,
His body gleams amid eternal snows,
His tears fall from the skies.

I see his face in every flower;
The thunder and singing of the birds
Are but his voice – and carven by his
    power,
Rocks are his written words.

All pathways by his feet are worn,
His strong heart stirs the ever-beating
    sea,
His crown of thorns is twined of every
    thorn,
His cross is every tree.

Joseph Mary Plunkett, 'Earthsong', from The Prose and
Poetry of England

Read Psalm 86

COLLECT

Thou passion-flower of virtues beloved,
Sanctified by the holy blood of the Lamb,

49

Son of Mary fair, Foster Son of Bride of
    Kine,
Son of Mary great, helpful Mother of the
    people.

There is no earth, no land,
There is no lake, no ocean,
There is no pool, no water,
There is no forest, no steep,
That is not to me full safe
By the protection of the passion-flower of
    virtues.

Carmina Gadelica II 115

CENTRING PRAYER

      'I see his face in every flower' –
      It is your face, O Lord, that I see;
      hide not your face.

Wilderness

God is in your heart yet you search for him in
the wilderness.   *Anon.*

The Call of the Wilderness

Therefore, behold I, God, will allure her,
and will lead her into the wilderness;
and I will speak to her heart . . .
and she shall sing there according to the
    days of her youth,
and according to the days of her coming
    up out of the land of Egypt.

And it shall be in that day, saith the
    Lord,
that she shall call me: *My Husband,*
and she shall call me no more *Baal* . . .
and I will espouse thee to me for ever;
and I will espouse thee to me in justice
    and judgement,
and in mercy and commiserations.
And I will espouse thee to me in faith;
and thou shalt know that I am the Lord.
           Hosea 2:14–20 DOUAI BIBLE

Read Psalm 18

I will take you from the nations:
and gather you from every country
and bring you home from your own land.

I will pour clean water upon you:
purify you from all defilement
and cleanse you from all your idols.

A new heart I will give you
and put a new spirit within you:
I will take from your body the heart of
    stone
and give you a heart of flesh.

I will put my spirit within you:
make you walk in my ways
and observe my decrees.

You shall dwell in the land
    I gave to your forebears:
you shall be my people
and I will be your God.

Glory to the Father and to the Son:
and to the Holy Spirit;
as it was in the beginning is now:
and shall be for ever. Amen.

Ezekiel 36:24–28

CENTRING PRAYER

> There is no place
> where God is not;
> wherever I go,
> there God is.
>
> *Anon.*

Rocks and Soil

> I arise today
> Through the strength of heaven;
> Light of the sun,
> Radiance of moon,
> Splendour of fire,
> Speed of lightning,
> Swiftness of wind,
> Depth of sea,
> Stability of earth,
> Firmness of rock.
> > *St Patrick, 'The Cry of the Deer'*

MEDITATION

> In God alone is my soul at rest;
> my help comes from him.
> He alone is my rock, my stronghold,
> my fortress; I stand firm.
>
> How long will you attack me
> to break me down,
> as though I were a tottering wall,
> or a tumbling fence?
>
> Their plan is only to destroy;
> they take pleasure in lies.
> With their mouth they utter blessing
> but in their heart they curse.
>
> In God alone be at rest, my soul;
> for my hope comes from him.
> He alone is my rock, my stronghold,
> my fortress, I stand firm.

In God is my safety and glory,
the rock of my strength.
Take refuge in God, all you people.
Trust in him at all times.
Pour out your hearts before him
for God is our refuge.

Common folk are only a breath,
the great are an illusion.
Placed in the scales, they rise;
they weigh less than a breath.

Do not put your trust in oppression
nor vain hopes on plunder.
Do not set your heart on riches
even when they increase.

For God has said only one thing;
only two do I know:
that to God alone belongs power
and to you, Lord, love;
and that you repay us all
according to our deeds.

Psalm 62 GRAIL

Read Psalm 27

COLLECT

Lord, help us to hear
The rock, the fish,
The beast, the bird,
The multitudinous
Elements
And be
Tender as the opening leaf
That answers to your call.
Euanie Tippett, 'Earthsong'

54

The earth is mother of all for contained
in her are the seeds of all.

Hildegard of Bingen[17]

WATER

May the Spirit satisfy you with the water of grace.

MEDITATION

For Holy Sprinkling at River or Well

Let us commend ourselves and each other to the grace and power of Jesus Christ, that the Lord may ease our suffering and grant us health and salvation.[18]

(a sign of the cross with water may be made on the forehead)

A small drop of water
To thy forehead, beloved,
Meet for the Father, Son and Spirit,
The Triune of power.

A small drop of water,
To encompass my beloved,
Meet for Father, Son and Spirit,
The Triune of power.

A small drop of water
To fill thee with each grace,
Meet for Father, Son and Spirit.
The Triune of power.

Carmina Gadelica III 22

Read Psalm 40

COLLECT

Lord in your mercy give us living water, always
springing up as a fountain of healing: free us,
body, mind and spirit from every danger and
admit us to your presence in purity of heart.
Grant this through Christ our Lord. Amen.

CENTRING PRAYER

> Out of the depths I cry to you, O Lord;
> O Lord, hear my voice.
>
> *Psalm 130:1*

Sea

Let us adore the Lord, maker of wondrous
works, great bright heaven with its angels, the
white-waved sea on the earth.   *from the Gaelic*

MEDITATION

O God, God of all men,
God of heaven and earth, sea and rivers,
God of sun and moon, of all the stars,
God of high mountains and of lowly
      valleys,
God over heaven, and in heaven, and
      under heaven.

He has a dwelling
in heaven and earth and sea
and in all things that are in them.

He inspires all things,
He quickens all things,
He is over all things,
He supports all things.

He makes the light of the sun to shine,
He surrounds the moon and stars,
and He has made wells in the arid earth,
placed dry islands in the sea
and stars for the service
of the greater luminaries.

He has a Son
coeternal with Himself, like to Himself;
not junior is Son to Father,
nor Father senior to the Son.

And the Holy Spirit
breathes in them;
not separate are Father
and Son and Holy Spirit.

St Patrick's Creed [19]

Read Psalm 93

COLLECT

May this journey be easy, may it be a
    journey of profit in my hands!
Holy Christ against demons, against
    weapons, against killings!

May Jesus and the Father, may the Holy
    Spirit sanctify us!
May the mysterious God be not hidden in
    darkness, may the bright King save us!

May the cross of Christ's body and Mary
    guard us on the road!
May it not be unlucky for us, may it be
    successful and easy!
Middle Irish, translated by Oliver Davies

CENTRING PRAYER

The rippling tide of LOVE flows secretly
    out from GOD into the SOUL
    —And it draws mightily back to its SOURCE
MECHTILD OF MAGDEBURG [20]

Ocean Blessing

FOCUS

Bless the Lord you whales and all that
   swim in the waters:
sing his praise and exalt him for ever.

Benedicite

MEDITATION

God the Father all-powerful, benign,
Jesu the Son of tears and of sorrow,
With thy co-assistance, O! Holy Spirit.

The Three—one, ever-living, ever-mighty,
   everlasting,
Who brought the Children of Israel
   through the Red Sea,
And Jonah to land from the belly of the
   great creature of the ocean.

When the storm poured on the Sea of
   Galilee,

Sain us and shield and sanctify us,
Be Thou, King of the elements, seated at
   our helm,
And lead us in peace to the end of our
   journey.

With winds mild, kindly, benign,
   pleasant,
Without swirl, without whirl, without
   eddy,
That would do no harmful deed to us.

We ask all things of Thee, O God,
According to Thine own will and word.

Carmina Gadelica I 329

Read Psalm 8

If I ascend up into heaven, thou art there: if I make my bed in hell, behold, thou art there. If I take the wings of the morning, and dwell in the uttermost parts of the sea; even there shall thy hand lead me, and thy right hand shall hold me.

Psalm 139:8–10

CENTRING PRAYER

> God is in the water,
> God is in the dry land,
> God is in the heart.

61

Rivers

> Into the sea all rivers go,
> and yet the sea is never filled,
> and still to their goal the rivers go.
>
> *Anon.*

MEDITATION

Like the deer that yearns
for running streams,
so my soul is yearning
for you, my God.

My soul is thirsting for God,
the God of my life;
when can I enter and see
the face of God?

My tears have become my bread,
by night, by day,
as I hear it said all the day long:
'Where is your God?'

These things will I remember
as I pour out my soul:
how would I lead the rejoicing crowd
into the house of God,
amid cries of gladness and thanksgiving,
the throng wild with joy.

Why are you cast down, my soul,
why groan within me?
Hope in God; I will praise him still,
my saviour and my God.

My soul is cast down within me
as I think of you,
from the country of Jordon and Mount
    Hermon,
from the Hill of Mizar.

Deep is calling on deep,
in the road of waters;
your torrents and all your waves
swept over me.

By day the Lord will send
his loving kindness;
by night I will sing to him,
praise the God of my life.

I will say to God, my rock:
'Why have you forgotten me?
Why do I go mourning
oppressed by the foe?'

With cries that pierce me to the heart,
my enemies revile me,
saying to me all the day long:
'Where is your God?'

Why are you cast down, my soul,
why groan within me?
Hope in God; I will praise him still,
my saviour and my God.

Psalm 42[21]

God is a great underground river
that no one can dam up
and no one can stop.

Meister Eckhart

63

Read Psalm 42

May the Father take you
In His fragrant clasp of love,
When you go across the flooding streams
And the black river of death.

Anon.

AIR

The air,
with its penetrating strength,
characterizes
the victorious banner that is trust.

It gives light
to the fire's flame
and sprinkles
the imagination of believers
with the dew of hope.

Thus does trust show the way.

Those who breathe this dew
long for heavenly things.
They carry within
    refreshing,
    fulfilling,
    greening love,
with which they hasten to the aid of all.

With the passion of heavenly yearning,
they produce rich fruit.

Hildegard of Bingen

GOD is Breath,
   for the breath of the wind is shared by all,
goes EVERYWHERE; nothing shuts it in,
     NOTHING holds it prisoner

MAXIMUS THE CONFESSOR

Ye hosts angelic
by the high archangels led,
with heavenly power beneficent,
mighty in the music of the Word:
Great ones entrusted with the
    sovereignty
of infinite celestial spheres
marshalling the Cherubim
and the flaming Seraphim;
Ye, O Michael Prince of Heaven,
and Gabriel by whom the word is given,
Raphael with healing ministry
(to those who yet in bondage are),
guide our footsteps as we journey
onward into Paradise.

St Martial (fourth century)

Wind

FOCUS

The wind blows where it wills; you hear the sound of it, but you do not know where it comes from or where it is going. So it is with everyone who is born from the Spirit.

John 3:8 R.E.B.

MEDITATION

See, cut in woods, through flood of twin-
   horned Rhine
passes the keel, and greased slips over
   seas –
   *Heave, men! And let resounding echo
   sound our 'heave'.*

The winds raise blasts, wild rain-storms
   wreck their spite
but ready strength of men subdues it all –
   *Heave, men! And let resounding echo
   sound our 'heave'.*

Clouds melt away and the harsh tempest
   stills,
effort tames all, great toil is conqueror –
   *Heave, men! And let resounding echo
   sound our 'heave'.*

Endure and keep yourselves for happy
   things;
you suffered worst, and these too God
   shall end –
   *Heave, men! And let resounding echo
   sound our 'heave'.*

Thus acts the foul fiend: wearing out the
    heart
and with temptation shaking inmost
    parts –
    You men, remember Christ with mind still
    sounding 'heave'.

Stand firm in soul and spurn the foul
    fiend's tricks
and seek defence in virtue's armoury –
    You men, remember Christ with mind still
    sounding 'heave'.
    Columbanus to his monks (translated from the Medieval
                       Irish by James Carney)

Read Psalm 103

COLLECT

Lord of fire, of wind and moon and waters. Protect us in tempest and in storm. Be with us on
our journey to your heavenly Kingdom where
you live and reign, One God, world without
end. Amen.

CENTRING PRAYER

Bless the Lord all winds that blow.

Birds

Have you not seen how all in the Heavens and in
the Earth utters the praise of God? – the very
birds as they spread their wings? Every creature knows its prayer and its praise, and God
knows what they do.   *Anon.*

MEDITATION

>Blackbird, it is well for you
>wherever in the thicket be your nest,
>hermit that sounds no bell,
>sweet, soft, fairylike is your note.[22]

>A wall of forest looms above
>and sweetly the blackbird sings;
>all the birds make melody
>over me and my books and things.

>There sings to me the cuckoo
>from bush-citadels in grey hood.
>God's doom! May the Lord protect me
>writing well, under the great wood.[23]

>Gay comes the singer
>With a song,
>Sing we all together,
>All things young;
>Field and wood and fallow,
>Lark at dawn,
>Young rooks cawing, cawing,
>Philomel
>Still complaining of the ancient wrong.

Twitters now the swallow,
Swans are shrill
Still remembering sorrow,
Cuckoo, cuckoo, goes the cuckoo calling
On the wooded hill.

The birds sing fair,
Shining earth,
Gracious after travail
Of new birth,
Lies in radiant light,
Fragrant air.

Broad spreads the lime,
Bough and leaf.
Underfoot the thyme,
Green the turf.
Here come the dances,
In the grass
Running water glances,
Murmurs past.

Happy is the place,
Whispering
Through the open weather
Blow the winds of spring.[24]

Read Psalm 104

COLLECT

All praise to Thee, my God, this day,
For all thy blessings on the way,
Keep me, O keep me, King of Kings,
Beneath Thy own Almighty wings.

CENTRING PRAYER

Bless the Lord all birds of the air.

Insects

FOCUS

Shall I, a gnat which dances in Thy ray dare to
be reverent?   *Coventry Patmore*

MEDITATION

Yet none among the birds is like the bee,
Who is the very type of chastity,
Save she who bore the burden that was
   Christ
In her inviolate womb.[25]

Last night did Christ the Sun rise from
   the dark,
The mystic harvest of the fields of God,
And now the little wandering tribes of
   bees
Are brawling in the scarlet flowers
   abroad.
The winds are soft with birdsong; all
   night long
Darkling the nightingale her descant
   told,
And now inside church doors the happy
   folk
The Alleluia chant a hundredfold.
O father of thy folk, be thine by right
The Easter joy, the threshold of the light.
      Sedulius Scottus, 'Easter Sunday'[26]

Read Psalm 65

Little beetle, little beetle,
Rememberest thou yesterday?
Little beetle, little beetle,
Rememberest thou yesterday?
Little beetle, little beetle,
Rememberest thou yesterday?
The Son of God went by?

Carmina Gadelica II 193

COLLECT

O God our Father, we thank you for the little things in life, and to notice them, and to remember them, for all creation lives and flows in ceaseless praise; for the sake of Christ, Lord of all Creation.

CENTRING PRAYER

Glory to God for all things!

FIRE

Do you wish to know my meaning?
Then lie down in the Fire.
See and taste the flowing Godhead
through your being.
Feel the Holy Spirit moving and
   compelling
you within the flowing Fire and
Light of God.

Mechtild of Magdeburg

According to the multitude of your mercies,
cleanse my iniquity.   *Psalm 51:1*

MEDITATION

O star-like sun,
O guiding light,
O home of the planets,
O fiery-maned and marvellous one,
O fertile, undulating, fiery sea,
   Forgive.

O fiery glow,
O fiery flame of Judgement,
   Forgive.

O holy story-teller, holy scholar,
O full of holy grace, of holy strength,
O overflowing, loving, silent one,
O generous and thunderous giver of gifts,
   Forgive.

73

O rock-like warrior of a hundred hosts,
O fair crowned one, victorious, skilled in
   battle,
      Forgive.
   Ciaran of Clonmacnois, 'Irish Litany' (sixth century)[27]

Read Psalm 97

The creative operation of God
does not simply mould us like soft clay.
It is a Fire that animates all it touches,
a spirit that gives life.
So it is in living
that we should give ourselves to that
creative action, imitate it, and
identify with it.
   Pierre Teilhard de Chardin, Mystical Milieu, 1917

COLLECT

Father, enable us to share in the light of your
glory through your Son, the light of the world.
Kindle in us the fire of your love, and inflame
us with new hope. Purify our minds and bring
us one day to the feast of eternal light. We ask
this through Christ our Lord. Amen.

Holy Spirit, Your fiery Love warms the
   whole earth.
Your Beauty blazes into sun and fire.
You radiate Glory within and without.
The flame of Your womanly Wisdom
   burns in the shrine of my soul.
The heat of Your Compassion melts my
   cold heart,
and penetrates my whole body's being.

I rest in Your radiance, and respond to
    Your calling,
filled with the Light of Your Divine
    Presence. Amen.

Anon. (twentieth century)

CENTRING PRAYER

> Bless O Lord the earth
> beneath my feet;
> bless the Lord
> you fire and heat.

Sun

In our pilgrimage we have received a sign that
we are now light, for we are still saved by hope
and children of the light and children of the
day, not children of night and darkness which
once we were.   *St Augustine,* Confessions *IV*

MEDITATION

Hail to thee, thou sun of the seasons,
As thou traversest the skies aloft;
Thy steps are strong on the wing of the
    heavens,
Thou art the glorious mother of the stars.

Thou liest down in the destructive ocean
Without impairment and without fear;
Thou risest up on the peaceful wave-crest
Like a queenly maiden in bloom.
                    Carmina Gadelica III 311

God, kindle Thou in my heart within
A flame of love to my neighbour,
To my foe, to my friend, to my kindred
    all,
To the brave, to the knave, to the thrall,
O Son of the loveliest Mary,
From the lowliest thing that liveth,
To the Name that is highest of all.
O Son of the loveliest Mary,
From the lowliest thing that liveth,
To the Name that is highest of all.
                    Carmina Gadelica I 231

Read Psalm 136

COLLECT

O Thou who givest sustenance to the universe, from whom all things proceed, to whom all things return, unveil to us the face of the true spiritual Sun hidden by a disc of golden light, that we may know the truth and do our whole duty as we journey to Thy sacred feet.

CENTRING PRAYER

> Glory to Thee,
> Thou glorious Sun.

Moon

Greeting to you, new moon, kindly jewel
of guidance!
I bend my knees to you, I offer you my
love.

I bend my knees to you, I raise my hands
to you, I lift up
my eye to you, new moon of the seasons.

Greeting to you, new moon, darling of my
love! Greeting
to you, new moon, darling of graces.

You journey on your course, you steer
the flood-tides, you
light up your face for us, new moon of
the seasons.

Queen of guidance, queen of good luck,
queen of my love,
new moon of the seasons!
Scottish Gaelic; traditional folk prayer[28]

MEDITATION

She of my love is the new moon,
The King of all creatures blessing her;
Be mine a good purpose
Towards each creature of creation.

Holy be each thing
Which she illumines;
Kindly be each deed
Which she reveals.

78

Be her guidance on land
With all beset ones;
Be her guidance on the sea
With all distressed ones.

May the moon of moons
Be coming through thick clouds
On me and on every mortal
Who is coming through affliction.

May the virgin of my love
Be coming through dense dark clouds
To me and to each one
Who is in tribulation.

May the King of grace
Be helping my hand
Now and for ever
Till my resurrection day.

Carmina Gadelica III 299

Read Psalm 148

COLLECT

O love rose on the thorn!
O hovering bee in the honey!
O pure dove in your being!
O glorious sun in your setting!
O full moon in your course!
From you, O God, I will never turn away.

CENTRING PRAYER

Bless the Lord sun and moon:
bless the Lord you stars of heaven.

Stars

O strong of heart go where the road
of ancient honour climbs.
Bow not your craven shoulders.
Earth conquered gives the stars.

Boethius

MEDITATION

Behold the Lightener of the stars
On the crests of the clouds,
And the choralists of the sky
Lauding Him.

Coming down with acclaim
From the Father above,
Harp and lyre of song
Sounding to Him.

Christ, Thou refuge of my love,
Why should not I raise Thy fame!
Angels and saints melodious
Singing to Thee.

Thou son of the Mary of graces,
Of exceeding white purity of beauty,
Joy were it to me to be in the fields
Of Thy riches.

O Christ my beloved,
O Christ of the Holy Blood,
By day and by night
I praise Thee.

Carmina Gadelica I45

Read Psalm 147

God put the world together out of
    various elements:
He empowered it with wind,
He illuminated and connected it with
    stars,
He tilled it with all manner of creation.
All this is to the glory of His name.
                                    Hildegard of Bingen

COLLECT

O thou transcendent,
Nameless, the fibre and the breath,
Light of the light, shedding forth
    universes, thou centre of them,
Thou mightier centre of the true, the
    good, the loving,
Thou moral, spiritual fountain –
    affection's source – thou reservoir,
(O pensive soul of me – O thirst
    unsatisfied – waitest not there?
Waitest not haply for us somewhere
    there the Comrade perfect?)
Thou pulse – thou motive of the stars,
    suns, systems,
That circling, move in order, safe,
    harmonious,
Athwart the shapeless vastness of space,
How should I think, how breathe a single
    breath, how speak, if, out of myself,
I could not launch, to those, superior
    universes?
                                    Walt Whitman

All things by immortal power,
Near and far,
Hiddenly to each other linked are,
That thou canst not stir a flower
Without troubling a star.

CENTRING PRAYER

There is no star in the sky,
but proclaims His goodness.
Jesu! meet it were to praise Him.

INSCAPE

For you
there is only one road
that can lead to God
and this is
fidelity:

to remain
constantly true to
yourself, to what
you feel
is
highest in you.
The road
will open

before you as
you go

TEILHARD DE CHARDIN

BODY

There is no race of men
But rose from one same spring.
One Father of them all,
To all things giving.
He gave the sun his beams,
The moon her crescent of light,
To earth He gave mankind,
Stars to the night.
Prisoner in body, soul
Besieged by heaven,
Mortality is sprung
From a noble stock.

Why bluster about race,
And brag of ancestry?
If you would look at that from whence
    you came,
  God that begot you,
    Not one
  Would prove a degenerate son
    Or cling
  To the evil thing,
Lest he should lose his way
To his primeval spring.

Boethius[29]

Touch

FOCUS

God hugs you.
You are encircled
by the arms
of the mystery of God.
Hildegard of Bingen

MEDITATION

The marvels of God
are not brought forth
from one's self.
Rather,
it is more like a chord,
a sound that is played.
The tone does not come
out of the chord itself,
but rather,
through the touch
of the musician.

I am, of course,
the lyre and harp
of God's kindness.
Hildegard of Bingen

Read Psalm 144

COLLECT

May the road rise to meet you,
May the wind be always at your back.
May the sun shine warm upon your face.
May the rain fall softly upon your fields.

Until we meet again,
May God hold you in the hollow of His
    hand.

Gaelic blessing

CENTRING PRAYER

Into your hands I commend my spirit.

Sound

FOCUS

As the Godhead strikes the note
Humanity sings;
The Holy Spirit is the harpist
And all the strings must sound
Which are strung in love.
Mechtild of Magdeburg

MEDITATION

When the earth with spring returning
    buds again,
And the branches in the woods again are
    green,
And the sweetness of all flowers is in the
    grass,
Lilts the nightingale all passionate with
    song,
With the thrilling of her tiny swelling
    throat,
Flings the prophecy of spring and
    summer tides.
Beyond all birds that sing, clearer than
    flutes ...
Filling the woods and every little copse,
Most glorious with the rapture of the
    Spring ...
The snarer in the green wood holds his
    peace.
The swan falls silent, and the shrilling
    flute.
So small art thou, to take us all with
    singing,

None gave that voice, unless the King of
    Heaven.

Fulbert of Chartres[30]

Read Psalm 47

COLLECT

My soul give praise to the Lord;
I will praise the Lord all my days,
make music to my God while I live.
    Amen.

CENTRING PRAYER

Praise the Lord all who give sound to His Name.

Smell

I am the breeze
that nurtures all things green,
I encourage blossoms to flourish
with ripening fruits.

Hildegard of Bingen

MEDITATION

Take thou this rose, O Rose,
Since Love's own flower it is,
And by that rose
Thy lover captive is.

Smell thou this rose, O Rose,
And know thyself as sweet
As dawn is sweet.

Look on this rose, O Rose,
And looking, laugh on me,
And in thy laughter's ring
The nightingale shall sing.

Kiss thou this rose, O Rose,
That it may know the scarlet of thy mouth.

O Rose, this painted rose
Is not the whole,
Who paints the flower
Paints not its fragrant soul.

MS of Benedictbeuern[31]

Read Psalm 45

COLLECT

Now we must praise the author of the heavenly
Kingdom, the Creator's power and counsel, the
deeds of the Father of glory; now he, the eternal
God, was the author of all the marvels – He,
who first gave to the sons of men the heaven for
a roof, and then, Almighty Guardian of mankind, created the earth.   *Caedmon*

CENTRING PRAYER

Praise God who sends us the scents of the earth!

Sight

Those who look to the Lord will win new strength
they will grow WINGS like eagles,
     they will RUN and not be weary
     they will MARCH on and
          not grow faint

ISAIAH 40·31

MEDITATION

Of all the animals in Saint Gregory's monastery, the most outstanding spiritual athlete was undoubtedly Brother Eagle.

He could gaze into the Light with unrecoiling eye. The sight of Brother Eagle surpassed that of all other birds. The rays of Light did not make him blink and he was able to mount up to a very great height, such was the fitness of his prayer. At the command of God, the Eagle was able to detach himself from earthly desires and pass over with the flight of the heart everything which passes away. His conversation was in heaven, his eyrie in places of high hope, so nourished was he with a desire for heavenly things. He did not wish to dwell in things below and so did not degrade his mind to low objects, or in the baseness of everyday affairs.

In Christ, in heaven, through prayer and by power of grace, he understood the scheme of life. His descent from on high to eat of the

Flesh of Christ in Communion was the indispensible nourishment for his mystical flights. For Brother Eagle the carcass of the Eucharist was a day's food for a day's journey. Through the Eucharist his mystical prayer was nourished and sustained.

It is easy to understand the beauty of Brother Eagle's questing spirit as he circled high above in the Light of God, gazing into that Light with unblinking eye. Turning his eye to earth he would see his sacred Prey transfixed by love on the cross and, plummeting to earth, he would seek the Food of the Body of Christ. Thus we are all lifted up to the Divine Nature when we see the grace of the scheme of life in His Flesh, and descend from on high like an eagle to its prey.

Brother Eagle loved the Lord and flew in His ways. The Lord was his light and his salvation, whom then could he fear? Thus enlightened he could not deviate from the right path and knew how to stay the course.

The vision of God was alone the true refreshment of his soul. Prayer was the wing which lifted him up. Ravished by the sweetness of contemplation, the movement of his soul seemed to be the contrary of repose, but, journeying toward God, it was in repose because it saw Him, still as if through a mist. Brother Eagle's desire for God was insatiable. When he would think Him absent, he would see Him; and when he felt Him present; he would not see Him. It was very difficult for Eagle to conceive positively and exactly the Divine Reality. He needed the Incarnate Flesh not only as the food for his flights but as contact with the Divine Reality he could not see.

He managed to banish a lot of the mist of his corruptible nature and see God to some degree and yet, 'if he did not as yet see what It is, he certainly learnt what It is not' (*Moralia* 5, 62), for, as Abbot Gregory told him, 'When the heart is hung aloft in the height of contemplation whatever it has power to see perfectly is not God ... in that only is there truth in what we know concerning God, when we are made sensible we cannot fully know anything concerning Him' (*Moralia* 5, 66).

But Brother Eagle would never have loved God if he had not, in some measure, known Him, and therefore, he never ceased to be confident. He knew that as long as he was at home in the body he would, in some way, be an exile. And although Brother Eagle could not look directly at God, so great was the brightness, he could see God's light, subdued and indistinct, but as much as he could take, powering him up by grace to soar in the shaft of its sunbeam towards the Light. Raised up by the force of sanctity and elevated by desire for God, Eagle persevered so as to meet his God, in the cloud of unknowing. Even so, the light dazzled him, and he could not remain in these heights. He was dazzled by what he perceived of God and was knocked back, as if by a violent blow. Down he tumbled like one struck by lightning, recoiled, wide-eyed, such was the immensity of disproportion between the love of Brother Eagle and the all-encompassing fire of the love of God.

With his eye still illumined by the bright coruscations of unencompassed light flashing on it, the Eagle landed in a heap on the ground. Having seen some traces of Truth before him, he was recalled to a sense of his own lowliness. Father Gregory had often taught him that 'Not even in the sweetness of inward contemplation does the mind remain fixed for long, in that, being made to recoil by the very immensity of the light, it is called back to itself. And when it tastes that inward sweetness it is on fire with love, it longs to mount above itself; yet it falls back in broken state to the darkness of its frailty' (*Moralia* 5, 58).

> *Brian Brendan O'Malley,* The Animals of St Gregory

Read Psalm 24

COLLECT

Be thou my vision, O Lord of my heart;
Naught be all else to me, save that thou art,
Thou my best thought, by day or by night,
Waking or sleeping, thy presence my light.
> *Traditional Irish*

CENTRING PRAYER

My Lord and my God.

Taste

O lovely rose on the thorn, thou art sweet as the grape. A flower of great delight yet the root of your constancy is in the Holy Spirit ever fresh and ever green. *Mechtild of Magdeburg*

MEDITATION

In the Refectory

Lord Christ, we pray thy mercy on our
　　table spread,
And what thy gentle hands have given thy
　　men
Let it by thee be blessed: whate'er we have
Came from thy lavish heart and gentle
　　hand,
And all that's good is thine, for thou art
　　good.
And ye that eat, give thanks for it to
　　Christ,
And let the words ye utter be only peace,
For Christ loved peace: it was himself that
　　said,
Peace I give unto you, my peace I leave
　　with you.
Grant that our own may be a generous
　　hand
Breaking the bread for all poor men,
　　sharing the food.
Christ shall receive the bread thou gavest
　　his poor,
And shall not tarry to give thee reward.

Alcuin[32]

Read Psalm 81

Taste and see that the LORD is good.
Happy are they who find refuge in him!
Fear the LORD, you his holy people;
those who fear him lack for nothing.
Princes may suffer want and go hungry,
but those who seek the LORD lack no good
thing.

Psalm 34:8–10 R.E.B.

CENTRING PRAYER

My spirit has become dry because it forgets to
feed on you.

St John of the Cross

Fatigue

FOCUS

Our earthly condition is essentially that of way-
farers, of incompleteness moving towards fulfil-
ment and therefore of struggle.   *Yves Congar*

MEDITATION

Lord,
just as a pilgrim who travels all day
without eating or drinking
is nearly overcome by weariness,
but at last comes upon a good Inn
and is well refreshed with food and drink,
so in the spiritual life
my soul wishes to renounce the love of the
    world
and love you, my God.
So I set myself to this,
but sometimes I pray and labour
in body and soul all day long
without feeling any comfort and joy.
Yet, Lord, you have pity on all your creatures
and you send me spiritual food
and comfort me with devotion as you see fit,
lest I perish, lose heart
or fall into depression and complaint.
                              Walter Hilton (1393)

Read Psalm 73

COLLECT

O God, Thou art my God alone;
early to Thee my soul shall cry,

a pilgrim in a land unknown,
a thirsty land whose springs are dry.

Yet through this rough and thorny maze
I follow close to Thee, my God;
Thy hand unseen upholds my ways;
I safely tread where Thou hast trod.

James Montgomery (1822)

CENTRING PRAYER

I love thee, O Lord my strength.

Psalm 18:1

Sickness and Pain

FOCUS

There is no coming to consciousness without
pain.

C. G. Jung

MEDITATION

The soul does as pilgrims do who have eagerly
    climbed to
the summit of a mountain: they descend
with care – lest they fall over a precipice.
So it is with the soul:
On fire with its long love,
overpowered by the embrace of the Holy
    Trinity,
it begins to sink
and to cool.
As the sun from its highest zenith
sinks down into the night,
thus also, do we sink,
soul and body. . . .

God has wounded me
close unto death.
If God leaves me unanointed
I could never recover.
    Even if all the hills flowed with healing oils,
    and all the waters contained healing
        powers,
    and all the flowers and all the trees,
    dripped with healing ointments,
    Still
    I could never recover.

Mechtild of Magdeburg

Go *with* the pain, let it take you. ... Open your palms and your body to the pain. It comes in waves like a tide, and you must be open as a vessel lying on the beach, letting it fill you up and then, retreating, leaving you empty and clear .... With a deep breath – it has to be as deep as the pain – one reaches a kind of inner freedom from pain, as though the pain were not yours but your body's. The spirit lays the body on the altar.   *Anne Morrow Lindbergh*

Read Psalm 54

COLLECT

> I am not eager, bold
> Or strong – all that is past.
> I am ready not to do,
> At last, at last!
> *St Peter Canisius (1521–97)*

CENTRING PRAYER

O Christ, bless and uphold all who are in pain or sickness this day.

Temptation

FOCUS

We learn by the bitter experience of temptation that the spiritual life is not a matter of devout feeling or mere desire to be good. It is through temptation that most of us comprehend how serious a matter it is – a very matter of life and death, involving struggles for survival which are fierce and primitive.

Reginald Somerset Ward (1881–1962)

MEDITATION

Brother Horse was an animal of beautiful proportions with supple, rippling muscles and a high prancing action which was both sensual and restrained. He gave the impression that through collection within himself, he could at any moment burst forth in extended movement of speed and power if he so wished. His habit, in common with all his brethren, was white but for those who witnessed him, it had the significance of holy purity.

With beautiful, deep-set, dark, velvet-like eyes, sleepy yet penetrating, he belied their somnolence with flashes of acute discernment; showing him to be a mystic who could apprehend spiritual truths beyond the understanding. His look was turned towards God, that of a creature before his Creator, to whom he owed his whole being. With all of his deep equine heart he surrendered himself to God in a forward movement which grew daily, moment by moment, so absorbed by Love did he become.

Through prayer, he knew himself very well and was aware of his tendency to lust. He gathered himself together and was restrained from wanton impulse by the bit of continence, and progressed under the impulsion of love. Guided by the reins of chastity he could enter into any situation without fear, for he was ridden by a Heavenly Horseman who knew how to open his horse's heart to others in love, so that it was at once vulnerable yet detached. In this way no matter what situation the Horse found himself in, he would respond to the word of his Master.

This word was a 'hidden word' which came to him by ways beyond the sound of speech. The utterance of the Spirit would sound silently in his heart. Through constant attention to this sounding of the Word, the beautiful, powerful, sensual Brother Horse became more and more pliable to the commands of his Rider and less attached to temporal things. His humility and detachment were such that when startled by the uproar of riotous thoughts, his reliance on his Master was at once swift and understanding. By gathering his thoughts together and offering them in obedience to right ordering, he kept himself still – no matter what the commotion. By remaining still to outward disturbance, Brother Horse learned to dwell in the secrecy of a silent heart.

Brian Brendan O'Malley, The Animals of St. Gregory

Read Psalm 32

O God that art the only hope of the
    world,
The only refuge for unhappy men,
Abiding in the faithfulness of heaven,
Give me strong succour in this testing
    place.
O King, protect thy man from utter ruin
Lest the weak faith surrender to the
    tyrant,
Facing innumerable blows alone.
Remember I am dust, and wind, and
    shadow,
And life as fleeting as the flower of grass,
But may the eternal mercy which hath
    shone
From time of old
Rescue thy servant from the jaws of the
    lion.
Thou who didst come from on high in the
    cloak of flesh,
Strike down the dragon with that two-
    edged sword
Whereby our mortal flesh can war with
    the winds
And beat down strongholds, with our
    Captain God.

A prayer of the Venerable Bede

Grant Lord, that I may not, for one moment,
admit willingly into my soul any thought contrary to thy love.   *E. B. Pusey (1800–82)*

Pleasure

He remains a fool his whole life long
Who loves not women, wine and song.
Martin Luther

Wine it is that gives life pleasure,
Yet 'tis naught in single measure!
Better it is thrice repeated,
And the fourth is rich conceited.
At the fifth, the mind's labyrinthine,
At the sixth, the body's supine.
Anon.

O happy hour
When one so debonair
Took life upon her,
So gay, so fine, so rare,
O shining hair,
Hair of gold!
Naught that is base
Could that heart ever hold.
There is none like her, none,
That forehead with its crown of hair,
And that dark brow
Arched after Iris' bow.

Snow white,
Rose red,
Her like
Not among a thousand shall you find her.
Full lips aglow
White teeth a-sparkle
Voice soft and slow
Slender hands and slender side

Throat, all beauty else beside,
So that gods designed her.

A spark of living fire
Down flying from her
Whom above all other
I most desire
Kindled my heart that now in ashes lies.
   O thou that Beauty's handmaid art,
    If thou wilt have no pity on my smart
   A living man now dies.
   O tender Phyllis,
If thou wilt have no care
For my despair,
Never shall my heart be still
   For never shall I rest
Till my lips close on thy lips are laid
   My head upon thy breast.

Carmina Burana[33]

Read Psalm 45

Come, Love!
   Sing on,
      let me hear you sing this song!
   Sing for joy
   and laugh
     for I the Creator
   am truly subject
     to all creatures.

Mechtild of Magdeburg

Where'er the Christian sun doth shine
you'll find lots of laughter and good red
   wine.

I've always found it so.
Benedicamus Domino.

H. Belloc

Prayer at Night

Fountain of light, Light, Source of light
   Hear our prayer.
Our dark sin put to flight,
   Seek us, kindly light.

Whose holy strength created man,
   Whose law condemned, whose love
      redeemed,
Be thou in all men Love and Law
   Omnipotent.

The labour of the day is done,
   And we are safe,
Beneath the covert of thy grace;
   We give thee praise.

The sun has left us, comes the dark,
   Shine out, O Sun,
Whose light is golden on the face
   Of the angel host.

Pour down thy radiant light
   On our dark dullard mind.
Kindle us with thy torch
   That we may burn.

From horror, lust and fear
   Guard thou our sleep,
And if we sleep not, may our eyes behold
   The citizens of God.

There'll come a time when brother
  speaks with brother,
There'll come a time when joy will feast
  on joy.
There is a time for all things; now for
  parting,
O Love that knows no end and no alloy.
                                    Alcuin[34]

MIND AND HEART

Longing for God

'This place has no use at all except as
   showing that God is lovable, loving
   and worthy of giving up your life for.
If we were teaching, people would say,
   "Yes, they're doing a fine job."
If we were healing the sick, "Yes,
   wonderful people."
We do nothing of any use to man or
   beast; our only purpose is to love and
   praise God. A wonderful waste of
   time.'

Father Giles, Monk of Pluscarden

MEDITATION

O God, you are my God, for you I long;
for you my soul is thirsting.
My body pines for you
like a dry weary land without water.
So I gaze on you in the sanctuary
to see your strength and your glory.

For your love is better than life,
my lips will speak your praise.
So I will bless you all my life,
in your name I will lift up my hands.

My soul shall be filled as with a banquet,
my mouth shall praise you with joy.

On my bed I remember you.
On you I muse through the night
for you have been my help;
in the shadow of your wings I rejoice.
My soul clings to you;
your right hand holds me fast.

Psalm 63:1–8

Ah, Lord God, thou holy lover of my soul, when
thou comest into my soul, all that is within me
shall rejoice. Thou art my glory and the exulta-
tion of my heart; thou art my hope and refuge
in the day of my trouble. Set me free from all
evil passions, and heal my heart of all inordi-
nate affections; that being inwardly cured and
thoroughly cleansed, I may be made fit to love,
courageous to suffer, steady to persevere. Nothing is sweeter than love, nothing more courageous, nothing fuller nor better in heaven and
earth; because love is born of God, and cannot
rest but in God, above all created things. Let
me love thee more than myself, nor love myself
but for thee; and in thee all that truly love
thee, as the law of love commandeth, shining
out from thyself. Amen.   *Thomas à Kempis*

COLLECT

Whom have I in heaven but thee: and there is
none upon earth that I desire in comparison of
thee.   *Psalm 73:24* B.C.P.

CENTRING PRAYER

Lord grant me everything that helps me
    on the way to you;
Lord, take away from me everything that
    hinders me on the way to you.
St Nicholas Flue

Suffering

Man has places in his heart which do not yet exist, and into them he enters suffering in order that they may have existence.   *Leon Bloy*

MEDITATION

For Those who Suffer

Suffering transforms, matures, and
instructs.
Suffering increases our capacities of love
and understanding.
All suffering makes us have something
in common with any of those who suffer.
It is a power of communion.

Undoubtedly, suffering sometimes
hardens us.
It does not necessarily bring us closer to
virtue.
But it always brings us closer to truth.

Suffering and death are the only
unavoidable obstacles
which compel the most mediocre man
to call himself into question, to detach
himself
from his existence, and to ask himself
what would permit him to transcend it.

What neither love, nor prayer, nor
poetry, nor art
could do for most people, only death and
suffering
are capable of demanding.

But maybe the day will come when love,
   art, and prayer
will have enough power over us so that
we might be exempt from suffering and
   death.

Louis Evely[35]

Read Psalm 27

COLLECT

Lord, you did not come to explain away my suffering or remove it. You came to fill it with
your presence. Be present to me, may my heart
so overflow with your love that I am able to
love you in return. Amen.

CENTRING PRAYER

Whoever loves much, does much.
Thomas à Kempis

Sorrow

> How else but through a broken heart
> May Lord Christ enter in?
> *Oscar Wilde, 'The Ballad of Reading Gaol'*

MEDITATION

> The deeper the sorrow, so much the more
> does a man feel himself as nothing,
> as less than nothing,
> and abatement of self-esteem is a sign
> that the sorrower is a seeker
> who begins to take note of God.
> In a worldly sense it is said that
> he is a poor soldier who does not hope
> to attain the highest rank;
> in a godly-sense the reverse is true:
> the less one believes in oneself,
> not as man in general
> or as being a man,
> but of himself as an individual man,
> not with respect to talents,
> but with respect to guilt –
> so much more distinct
> will God become in him.
>
> *Søren Kierkegaard*[36]

And God shall wipe away all tears from their eyes; and there shall be no more death, neither sorrow, nor crying, neither shall there be any more pain: for the former things are passed away.   *Revelations 21:4* A.V.

114

Read Psalm 88

A stronghold in times of distress
they trust in you who cherish you.
For you forsake not those who seek you
   O Lord:
for the needy shall not always be
   forgotten
Nor shall the hope of the afflicted forever
   perish.

Psalm 9:10–11, 18

CENTRING PRAYER

. . . in spite of all,
Some shape of beauty moves away the
   pall
From our dark spirits.

John Keats, 'Endymion', Book I

Discouragement/Trust

We could never learn to be brave and patient if there were only joy in the world.   *Helen Keller*

MEDITATION

The Road Ahead

My Lord God,
I have no idea where I am going.
I do not see the road ahead of me.
I cannot know for certain where it will
    end . . . .
Nor do I really know myself,
and the fact that I think that I am
    following
your will does not mean that I am
    actually doing so.
But I believe that the desire to please
    you does in fact please you.
And I hope I have that desire in all that I
    am doing.
I hope that I will never do anything apart
    from that desire.
And I know that if I do this,
you will lead me by the right road though
    I may know nothing about it.
Therefore will I trust you always though
    I may seem lost in the shadow of death.
I will not fear, for you are ever with me,
and you will never leave me to face my
    perils alone.

      Thomas Merton, quoted in Prayers for Pilgrims,
      ed. Margaret Pawley

Read Psalm 30

> He who would valiant be
> 'Gainst all disaster,
> Let him in constancy
> Follow the Master.
> There's no discouragement
> Shall make him once relent
> His first avowed intent
>   To be a pilgrim.
>
> Who so beset him round
> With dismal stories,
> Do but themselves confound –
> His strength the more is.
> No foes shall stay his might,
> Though he with giants fight:
> He will make good his right
>   To be a pilgrim.
>
> Since, Lord, thou dost defend
> Us with thy Spirit,
> We know we at the end
> Shall life inherit.
> Then fancies flee away!
> I'll fear not what men say,
> I'll labour night and day
>   To be a pilgrim.
>   *John Bunyan (1628–88) and*
>   *Percy Dearmer (1867–1936)*[37]

CENTRING PRAYER

> I will love thee, O Lord, my strength.
>   *Psalm 18:1*

117

Depression

FOCUS

It is not easy to find happiness in
  ourselves,
and it is not possible to find it elsewhere.
                                    Agnes Repplier

MEDITATION

Alas, his mind is sunk,
Plunged headlong deep,
The inner light gone out, and now
His face is to the dark that lies without.
Anxiety that's poisonous swells higher
With every gust of earth
Till it fills the vast.
The man that used to wander through
  free heaven,
And knew its windings,
That looked upon the redness of the sun
And saw the stars that wait on the cold
  moon,
Each travelling star that wheeled and
  turned
Through the several spheres.
He held her captive in his poetry,
What secret stirs the sounding winds
That they must still be harrying the sea;
What spirits whirls the solid-standing
  world
And why the sun that rose in the bright
  East
Must sink at evening in the Western sea;

What tempers the still hours of a day in
    spring,
And brings to earth the rose,
And by what mystery of vintages
Autumn decants the heavy swelling
    grapes
In the year's close.
These were his poetry: he loved to rhyme
Earth's secret source and spring.
But the light of his mind has dimmed,
He lies there, heavy chains about his
    neck,
Their weight has bowed his head, so that
    his face
Is downward, and his eyes
Gaze but on sullen earth.

                                   Boethius[38]

Read Psalm 102

COLLECT

Lead, kindly light, amid the encircling gloom,
    Lead thou me on;
The night is dark, and I am far from home,
    Lead thou me on.
Keep thou my feet; I do not ask to see
The distant scene; one step enough for me.

I was not ever thus, nor prayed that thou
    Shouldst lead me on;
I loved to choose and see my path; but now
    Lead thou me on.
I loved the garish day, and, spite of fears,
Pride ruled my will: remember not past years.

So long thy power hath blest me, sure it still
  Will lead me on
O'er moor and fen, o'er crag and torrent, till
  The night is gone,
And with the morn those angel faces smile,
Which I have loved long since, and lost
  awhile.

John Henry Newman (1801–90) [39]

CENTRING PRAYER

LORD
I BELIEVE
HELP THOU MINE
UNBELIEF

MARK 9·24. A·V

Separation

He who is joined with all the living has hope.

Ecclesiastes 9:4 R.S.V.

MEDITATION

Separation from Those we Love

Nothing can fill the gap when we are away from those we love, and it would be wrong to try and find anything. We must simply hold out and win through. That sounds very hard at first, but at the same time it is a great consolation, since leaving the gap unfilled preserves the bonds between us. It is nonsense to say that God fills the gap; he does not fill it, but keeps it empty so that our communion with another may be kept alive, even at the cost of pain.

Dietrich Bonhoeffer [40]

Read Psalm 22

COLLECT

Come, make an end of singing and of grieving,
But not an end of love.
I wrote this song, beloved, bitter weeping,
And yet I know 'twill prove
That by God's grace,
We two shall see each other face to face,
And stand together with a heart at rest.

Alcuin

CENTRING PRAYER

Lord, my heart is restless until it rests in Thee.

121

Anxiety

Anxiety does not empty tomorrow of its sorrows, but only empties today of its strength.

Charles Spurgeon

O sorrow, that art still Love's company,
Whose griefs abide with me,
And have no remedy,
Sorrow doth drive me: how else should it
   be?
I go to exile from my darling one;
There is none like her, none,
Had Paris seen her, Helen were alone.

O valley, still be gay,
Valley with roses climbing all the way,
Among all valleys one,
Valley the fairest that is in the hills.
Soft on thee shines the sun,
Softly the moon; the birds
Sing rare for thee. O valley, be thou fair!
Yea, for the sick at heart find solace
   there.

MS of Benedictbeuern [41]

MEDITATION

To Meet Whatever Comes

We ask God that you may receive from him all wisdom and spiritual understanding for full insight into his will, so that your manner of life may be worthy of the Lord and entirely pleasing to him. We pray that you may bear fruit in active goodness of every kind, and grow in the knowledge of God. May he strengthen you, in his glorious might, with ample power to meet whatever comes with fortitude, patience and joy; and to give thanks to the Father who has made you fit to share the heritage of God's people in the realm of light.   *Colossians 1:9–12* N.E.B.

Therefore do not be anxious about tomorrow,
for tomorrow will be anxious for itself.
Let the day's own trouble
be sufficient for the day.

Matthew 6:34

Read Psalm 28

COLLECT

God, give us grace to accept with serenity the things that cannot be changed; courage to change the things that should be changed; and the wisdom to distinguish the one from the other.   *Reinhold Niebuhr*

CENTRING PRAYER

Father,
I am seeking:
I am hesitant and uncertain,
but will you, O God,
watch over each step of mine
and guide me.

St Augustine

Courage

FOCUS

COURAGE
IS GRACE UNDER PRESSURE

ERNEST HEMINGWAY

MEDITATION

Father, hear the prayer we offer:
Not for ease that prayer shall be,
But for strength that we may ever
Live our lives courageously.

Not for ever in green pastures
Do we ask our way to be;
But the steep and rugged pathway
May we tread rejoicingly.

Not for ever by still waters
Would we idly rest and stay;
But would smite the living fountains
From the rocks along the way.

Be our strength in hours of weakness,
In our wanderings be our guide;
Through endeavour, failure, danger,
Father, be thou at our side.

Love Maria Willis (1824–1908)[42]

Read Psalm 101

COLLECT

> Do not be afraid to throw yourself on the
>   Lord!
> He will not draw back and let you fall!
> Put your worries aside and throw
>   yourself on him:
> He will welcome you and heal you.
>
> *St Augustine,* Confessions *VIII, 11*

CENTRING PRAYER

> O search me, God, and know my heart.
> O test me and know my thoughts.
>
> *Psalm 139:23*

Happiness/Laughter

Those who joy would win must share it; happiness was born a twin.   *Lord Byron*

MEDITATION

Holy Christ Child
You smile sunrise into the sky.
You laugh the flowers into bloom.
Your holy play brings this day into being,
and renews all creation.
I come to You in trust like a little child.
I breathe Your love deeply into my being.
I see You in all with a child's wondering
    eyes,
And I ask You, Divine Child, to let me play
    this day with You,
laughing, trusting, delighting, creating;
and so by Your grace, with great gladness,
enter the realm of Heaven. Amen.
                    Anon. (twentieth century)

Read Psalm 127

COLLECT

My Lord and God,
the words of Your Spirit are laden with
    delights.
As often as I hear them, my soul seems to
    absorb them
and they enter the heart of my body like
    the most delicious food,

126

bringing unbounded joy and unspeakable
  comfort.

After hearing Your words, I remain both
  satisfied and hungry –
satisfied, for I desire nothing else;
but hungry, for I crave more of Your
  words.

St Bridget of Sweden

CENTRING PRAYER

Happy the one who walks in the way of
  the Lord –
who is happy through You alone.

SPIRIT

An American Indian's Prayer to God

O Great Spirit
whose voice I hear in the winds,
and whose breath gives life to the world,
hear me.

I come to you as one of your many children.
I am small and weak.
I need your strength and your wisdom.

May I walk in beauty.
Make my eyes ever behold the red and purple
  sunset.
Make my hands respect the things you have
  made,
and my ears sharp to hear your voice.

Make me wise so that I may know
the things you have taught your children,
the lessons you have hidden in every leaf and
  rock.

Make me strong
so that I may not be superior to other people,
but able to fight my greatest enemy,
which is myself.

Make me ever ready to come to you with
  straight eyes
so that, when life fades as the fading sunset,
my spirit may come to you without shame.

Joy

True joy is not an emotional state. It is not that
which one feels when some desire is satisfied,
or when everything at last goes well. It is
inward; it is of the soul.   *Donald Walters*[43]

MEDITATION

Be Joyful in the Lord All You Lands

The Psalmist says: 'Be joyful in the Lord all
you Lands!' Have all the lands heard this
invitation? Yes, all the lands have heard this
invitation. Already all the lands are making a
joyful noise to the Lord. If one part is not yet
praising him, it soon will.

The Church going out from Jerusalem is
spread out among all peoples. The good are
mixed in with the wicked. Through the mouth
of the wicked all the lands are murmuring
against the Lord: through the mouth of the
good all the lands are making a joyful noise to
the Lord.

And what is this joyful noise? Another Psalm
exclaims: 'Blessed are the people who know the
festal shout!' (Psalm 89:16). It must then be
something very important if the experience of
it brings happiness. Let us run towards this happiness, let us take careful note how to achieve
this joyful noise.

One who is making a joyful noise does not
utter words. No words are needed to make his
joy heard. It is the song of a soul overflowing

with joy, expressing its feelings as it may, above the level of discourse.

We find ourselves in this state of jubilation when we are glorifying God and we feel incapable of speaking of him – when for example we are considering the whole creation which makes itself available for us to know and to act in. The soul then asks: 'Who has made all this? And who has put me here? What are these truths that I am understanding? And who am I that understands? Who is it who has made it all? Who is he?'

If you want some idea of who he is, you must draw nearer to him. To look from a distance is to risk being deceived. It is the spirit that perceives him and the heart that sees him. What sort of heart? 'Blessed are the pure in heart: they shall see God' (Matthew 5:8).

You must draw nearer to him by becoming like him. You will feel his presence to the extent that love grows in you, because God is Love.

Then you will not be able to do anything but praise him. And if you make a joyful noise to the Lord, you will understand the joyful noise that all the lands make to him.   *St Augustine*[44]

Read Psalm 98

COLLECT

Let us pray for the fruit of the Spirit.

The harvest of the Spirit is love, joy, peace, good temper, gentleness, goodness, humility and self-control. Produce in us thy harvest, O Holy Spirit.

Blest Holy Spirit.   *George Appleton*[45]

CENTRING PRAYER

He who bends to himself a joy
Does the winged life destroy;
But he who kisses the joy as it flies
Lives in eternity's sunrise.

William Blake

Peace

FOCUS

The dayspring has dawned upon us from on
   high
to give light to those who live in darkness
and to guide our feet into the way of peace.

Just as the bread which we break was
   scattered over the earth,
was gathered in and became one,
bring us together from everywhere into the
   kingdom of your peace.

Epistle to Diognetus

MEDITATION

Across the hills and through the valley's shade,
   Alone the small script goes,
Seeking for Benedict's beloved roof,
   Where waits its sure repose.
They come and find, the tired travellers,
   Green herbs and ample bread,
Quiet and brothers' love and humbleness,
   Christ's peace on every head.
'Written to Paul the Deacon at Monte Cassino'[46]

Read Psalm 46

COLLECT

O God, source of everything divine,
You are good surpassing everything
   good, and just surpassing everything
   just.

132

In you is tranquillity, as well as peace
   and harmony.
Heal our divisions and restore us to the
   unity of love
which is similar to Your divine nature.
Let the bonds of love and the ties of
   divine affection
make us one in the Spirit by Your peace
which renders everything peaceful.
                    St Dionysius of Alexandria (c. 200–65)

CENTRING PRAYER

   . . . follow the things that make for peace.
                              Romans 14:19

AFTERWORD

True love of God is a river of peace, streaming
out in its greatness and flowing in with gentle
waters. At the same time it is a torrent, rushing
along with mighty force and sweeping everything away with it.   *John of Ford*

Silence

The love of God is born in man by grace, fed with
the milk of reading, nourished with the food of
meditation, strengthened and enlightened by
prayer.   *William of St Thierry*

MEDITATION

> O happy, most happy the soul
> that is drawn by grace to God by God,
> so that, through the unity of the Spirit in
>   God,
> it takes no thought of itself,
> loving none but God and loving itself
>   only in God.
> 'Keep them in my name, whom thou hast
>   given me;
> that they shall be one as we also are'
>   (John 17:2).
> This is the end,
> this is the consummation,
> perfection, peace, the joy of God,
> the joy in the Holy Ghost:
> this is *silence in heaven*.
>
>   *William of St Thierry*

Cistercian contemplation, so far as I can understand it, has little in common with the complex
processes recorded in the writings of the great
mystics; for a humble and completely unintel-
lectual simplicity is one of the characteristics
of the Trappist order. Their contemplative sys-
tem consists mainly of the dedication of every

action, and of every second, to God. With time and practice, this permanent concentration of the mind upon God brings a full reward: peace of the soul, a kind of divine ravishment, an unspeakable happiness that a French Trappist writer describes as a prolonged intimation of Paradise.   *Patrick Leigh Fermor*[47]

Read Psalm 23

COLLECT

> Eternal King, grant me true quietness
> For thou art rest and quiet without end.
> Eternal light, grant me the abiding light,
> And may I live and quicken in thy good.
>   *Angilbert's prayer*

> *Love silence*
> it brings us near the fruit
> which the tongue is too weak to interpret.

> *From silence*
> something is born
> which draws us towards deeper silence.

> May God grant us to perceive
> that which is born in silence.
>   *St Isaac of Nineveh*

To every thing there is a season, and a time to every purpose under the heaven ... a time to keep silence, and a time to speak.
                    Ecclesiastes 3:1, 7

CENTRING PRAYER

> Go placidly amidst the noise
> and the haste . . .
> and remember what peace
> there may be in silence.
> *Max Ehrmann*

Contemplation

Love is the fountain of life,
and the soul which does not drink from it
cannot be called alive.

Bernard of Clairvaux

He who with his whole soul, desires God, certainly possesses the one he loves.

St Gregory the Great

MEDITATION

The Jesus Prayer: The Power of the Name

What shall we say of this divine prayer, in invocation of the Saviour, 'Lord Jesus Christ, Son of God, have mercy upon me'?

It is a prayer and a vow and a confession of faith, conferring upon us the Holy Spirit and divine gifts, cleansing the heart, driving out devils. It is the indwelling presence of Jesus Christ within us, and a fountain of spiritual reflections and divine thoughts. It is remission of sins, healing of soul and body, and shining of divine illumination; it is a well of God's mercy, bestowing upon the humble revelations and initiation into the mysteries of God. It is our only salvation, for it contains within itself the saving Name of our God, the only Name upon which we call, the Name of Jesus Christ the Son of God. 'For there is none other name under heaven given among men, whereby we must be saved,' as the Apostle says (Acts 4:12).

That is why all believers must continually confess this Name: both to preach the faith and as testimony to our love for the Lord Jesus Christ, from which nothing must ever separate us; and also because of the grace that comes to us from His name, and because of the remission of sins, the healing, sanctification, enlightenment, and, above all, the salvation which it confers. The Holy Gospel says: 'These are written, that ye might believe that Jesus is the Christ, the Son of God.' See, such is faith. And the Gospel adds, 'that believing ye might have life through his Name' (John 20:31). See, such is salvation and life.   *St Simeon of Thessalonica*

The Simplicity of the Jesus Prayer

The practice of the Jesus Prayer is simple. Stand before the Lord with the attention in the heart, and call to Him: 'Lord Jesus Christ, Son of God, have mercy on me!' The essential part of this is not in the words, but in faith, contrition, and self-surrender to the Lord. With these feelings one can stand before the Lord even without any words, and it will still be prayer.

Theophan the Recluse[48]

Read Psalm 84

CENTRING PRAYER

> Lord Jesus Christ
> Son of God
> Have mercy on me,
> A sinner.

What I do is live,
How I pray is breathe.
Thomas Merton

Compunction

There is only one life and that is God's life
which he gives us from moment to moment,
drawing us to himself with every breath we
take.   *Merton's* Palace of Nowhere

MEDITATION

What do locusts, which injure the fruits of men
more than any other smaller animals, show,
but the tongues of flatterers, which corrupt the
minds of earthly men, if they even observe
them producing any good fruits, by praising
them too immoderately?

St Gregory the Great, Moralia *31, 47*

After the well-known incident when Abbot
Gregory saw the English slave-boys in the mar-
ket at Rome, he himself wanted to go to convert
the English and obtained permission from the
Pope, Pelagius II, to do so. After three days'
journey, however, he and his party of monks
were resting by the roadside when a locust
settled on the book Gregory was reading.
'Locusta!' he exclaimed, 'loco sta!' – that is,
'stay in the place'; and, thus reminded of the
monastic principle of stability, he concluded
that it was not God's will that he should make
the journey to England.

Brother Locust, after a lifetime as a flatterer,
had also sought stability when he flew to the
Word as it lay open on Gregory's knee, and so
he too returned to Rome and entered the monas-

tery of the animals. He was often referred to by his brethren as a 'machine'. Perhaps it was because of his plated external skeleton or his legs which were like pistons or like saws; but more probably it was because Abbot Gregory had often called compunction a machine, and Brother Locust was compunctious. He was possessed by that nostalgia which accompanies the purer joys of contemplation. He was humble and, unlike the Ostrich, was not proud of it. Because of his past life he held himself to be abominable not only to the eye of the beholder but also to the eye of his own heart. This feeling accompanied him however high he leapt because the weight of his unworthy body always brought him tumbling down again. The force of love drove the engine of his soul which drew him out of the world and lifted him on high by the downward thrust of compunction. This compunction was indeed the machine whereby he exercised his love.

Love and compunction were the two realities of Brother Locust's spiritual life. In him they were an attitude rather than virtues, because his whole demeanour was that bow of reverence before the Divine Majesty of God, on recognizing the dependence of his whole being. Locust's humility showed itself in tears of sorrow for his failures in loving God and his neighbour as he ought; a pierced and smarting heart and an abiding sorrow for the ravages of his sin. And not only tears of sorrow but also prayer before the beauty and grandeur of God, a deep sentiment which melted into tears of joy.

Compunction means 'pricking' and what do

141

you think pricked the Locust's heart? A sword of the spirit which is the word of God. The word of God is alive and active. It cuts more keenly than any two-edged sword, piercing as far as the place where life and spirit, joints and marrow divide. It sifts the purposes and thoughts of the heart. There is nothing in creation that can hide from it; everything lies naked and exposed to the eyes of the One with whom we have to reckon (Hebrews 4:12–13).

Father Gregory taught Brother Locust four ways towards an attitude of compunction, the means to prayer, the condition of which is reached by the penetration of four arrows:

Arrow 1: Where are you? Sorrow for past infidelity.
Arrow 2: Where will you be? No one can be certain whether he will be worthy of love.
Arrow 3: To whom are you going? Prepare yourself.
Arrow 4: Where are you not? Desire for God and the blessed home from which you are absent.

Brother Locust found this fourth condition to be very similar to his own, as he hungered for the vision of the face of God. Locust's stung conscience was the wellspring of joy as well as sadness, for through his desire for God good was being drawn out of him, so that he experienced confidence, trust and security.

Brian Brendan O'Malley, The Animals of St. Gregory

Read Psalm 43

COLLECT

O Saviour Christ, who in great heaviness of soul before thy passion, didst fall down in prayer to thy heavenly father; give us grace that we also in all the troubles of this world, may run ever-more by most humble and instant prayer unto the aid and comfort of our heavenly Father, for thy name's sake.   *Primer of 1559*

CENTRING PRAYER

> Here is my heart, O God,
> here it is with all its secrets;
> look into my thoughts,
> O my hope,
> and take away all my wrong feelings:
> let my eyes ever be on you
> and release my feet from the snare.
>> *St Augustine,* Confessions *IV, 6*

> O Lord make haste to help me.

Perseverance

A pilgrim
travelling on a road where he has never
   been before
believes every house he sees from afar is
   the inn;
and not finding it, directs his belief to
   another;
and so from house to house
until he comes to the inn.
In the same way our soul,
as soon as she begins
the new, never yet made, journey of life,
directs her eyes
toward the goal of her supreme good
and whatever she sees
that appears to have some good in it
she thinks to be it.

Dante Alighieri

MEDITATION

The Lord, Our Protector – a Pilgrimage Song

I lift up my eyes to the mountains;
from where shall come my help?
My help shall come from the Lord
who made heaven and earth.

May he never allow you to stumble!
Let him sleep not, your guard.
No, he sleeps not nor slumbers,
Israel's guard.

The Lord is your guard and your shade;
at your right side he stands.
By day the sun shall not smite you
nor the moon in the night.

The Lord will guard you from evil,
he will guard your soul.
The Lord will guard your going and
    coming
both now and for ever.

Psalm 121

COLLECT

O Father, give the spirit power to climb
To the fountain of all light, and be
    purified.
Break through the mists of earth, the
    weight of the clod,
Shine forth in splendour, Thou that art
    calm weather,
And quiet resting place for faithful souls.
To see Thee is the end and the beginning,
Thou carriest us, and Thou dost go
    before,
Thou art the journey, and the journey's
    end.

Boethius

CENTRING PRAYER

**Blessed are those who
find their strength in you,
whose hearts are set on pilgrimage**

PSALM 84·5

> Come to the edge
> He said. They said:
> We are afraid.
> Come to the edge
> He said. They came.
> He pushed them, and
> they flew.
> > *Guillaume Apollinaire*

Love

To believe in him is to go to him by loving him.
William of St Thierry

Insomuch as love grows in you so in you beauty
grows. For love is the beauty of the soul.
St Augustine

The Beatific Vision

Betwixt the dawning and the day it came
   Upon me like a spell,
   While tolled a distant bell,
A wondrous vision but without a name
In pomp of shining mist and shadowed flame,
   Exceeding terrible;
Before me seemed to open awful Space,
   And sheeted tower and spire
   With forms of shrouded 'tire
Arose and beckoned with unearthly grace,
I felt a Presence though I saw no face
   But the dark rolling fire.

And then a Voice as sweet and soft as tears
   But yet of gladness part,
   Thrilled through my inmost heart,
Which told the secret of the solemn years
And swept away the clouds of gloomy fears,
   The riddles raised by art;
Till all my soul was bathed with trembling joy
   And lost in dreadful bliss,
   As at God's very kiss,
While the earth shrivelled up its broken toy,
And like a rose the heavens no longer coy
   Laid bare their blue abyss.

I knew with sudden insight all was best,
　　The passion and the pain,
　　The searching that seem vain
But lead if by dim blood-stained steps to Rest,
And only are the beatings of God's Breast
　　Beneath the iron chain;
I knew each work was blessèd in its place.
　　The eagle and the dove,
　　While nature was the glove
Of that dear Hand which everywhere we trace,
I felt a Presence though I saw no face,
　　And it was boundless Love

Frederick William Orde Ward

COLLECT

Friends, let us love one another, for love comes
from God and everyone who loves is begotten
by God and knows God. Anyone who does not
love can never have known God, for God is love.

1 John 4:7–9

Read Psalm 150

CENTRING PRAYER

The person who loves God is with God to the
extent that he loves.

St Bernard

AFTERWORD

From the fullness of joy the Father utters the
whole of himself to the Son, and in the same
way the Son, together with the Father, utters
the whole of himself to the Holy Spirit, so that
these three are one single font of love.

John of Ford on the Song of Songs 14:4

Wisdom

FOCUS

> I, the fiery life of divine wisdom,
> I ignite the beauty of the plains,
> I sparkle the waters,
> I burn in the sun,
>   and the moon,
>   and the stars.
> With wisdom I order all rightly.
> Above all I determine truth.
>
> *Hildegard of Bingen*

MEDITATION

Happy is the man that findeth wisdom,
and the man that getteth understanding.

For the gaining of it is better than the
    gaining of silver;
and the profit thereof than fine gold.

She is more precious than rubies:
And none of the things thou canst desire
    are to be compared with her. . . .

Her ways are ways of pleasantness,
and all her paths are peace.

Proverbs 3:13–15, 17

Blessed are You, my God,
for You open Your servants' hearts to
    knowledge,
render all their actions just,
and accomplish for their children
the plan that You have formed
with respect to those whom You have
    chosen.

149

May they remain unceasingly in Your
  presence!

How can one walk a stright path without
  Your help?

What can one accomplish without Your
  accord?

From You alone comes all knowledge.

Nothing takes place except in accord
  with Your will.

No one but you can make answer to You,
unravel the skein of Your sacred designs,
scrutinize Your unfathomable mysteries,
or meditate on Your astounding works
and the munificence of Your power.

Dead Sea Scrolls (20 BC to AD 70)

Read Psalm 1 or Psalm 119:89–112

COLLECT

> O Gracious and Holy Father, give us
>   Wisdom to perceive thee,
>   Diligence to seek thee,
>   Patience to wait for thee,
>   Eyes to behold thee,
>   A heart to meditate upon thee,
>   And a life to proclaim thee;
> Through the power of the Spirit of
> Jesus Christ our Lord. Amen.

St Benedict

CENTRING PRAYER

May the Holy Spirit of all Wisdom lead us ever
more deeply into Truth, that we may walk stead-
fastly in the ways of justice and love.

ARRIVAL

GOD
has given me the power
to change my ways

MECHTILD OF MAGDEBURG

Arrival

> God has given me
> the power
> to change my ways.
> *Mechtild of Magdeburg*

MEDITATION

Bring us, O Lord God,
at our last awakening in to the house and
　　gate of heaven,
to enter in to that gate and dwell in that
　　house,
where there shall be no darkness nor dazzling,
　　but one equal light;
　　no noise nor silence,
　　but one equal music;
　　no fears nor hopes,
　　but one equal possession;
　　no ends nor beginnings,
　　but one equal eternity;
in the habitations of thy majesty and thy
　　glory,
　　world without end.

John Donne

Read Psalm 122

COLLECT

May He support us all the day long, till the
shades lengthen, and the evening comes, and
the busy world is hushed, and the fever of life

is over, and the work is done! Then in His mercy may He give us a safe lodging, and a holy rest, and peace at the last.

John Henry Newman

CENTRING PRAYER

I said to the Man who stood at the Gate of the Year

Give me
a light that I may
tread safely into the
unknown. And he replied,
Go out into the darkness
and put your hand
into the hand of God.
That shall be to you
better than light
and safer
than a known
way

M·L·HASKINS

154

Consolation

I am serene because I know thou lovest me.
Because thou lovest me, naught can move me
from my peace. Because thou lovest me, I am as
one to whom all good has come.

From the Gaelic, translated by Alistair Maclean

MEDITATION

Never weather-beaten sail more willing
    bent to shore,
Never tired pilgrim's limbs affected
    slumber more,
Than my wearied spirit now longs to fly
    out of my troubled breast:
O come quickly, sweetest Lord, and take
    my soul to rest!

Ever blooming are the joys of heaven's
    high paradise,
Cold age deafs not there our ears, nor
    vapour dims our eyes;
Glory there the sun outshines, whose
    beams the blessed only see;
O come quickly, glorious Lord, and raise
    my spirit to thee!

Thomas Campion

Heal us
Grandfather,
Look at our brokenness.

We know that in all creation
Only the human family
Has strayed from the Sacred Way.

155

We know that we are the ones
Who are divided
And we are the ones
Who must come back together
To walk in the Sacred Way.

Grandfather,
Sacred One,
Teach us love, compassion, and honour
That we may heal the earth
And heal each other.

Read Psalm 100

COLLECT

I find Thee enthroned in my heart, my Lord
Jesus. It is enough. I know that Thou art
enthroned in heaven. My heart and heaven are
one.   *From the Gaelic, translated by Alistair Maclean*

CENTRING PRAYER

> On you, LORD, I fix my hope;
> You, LORD my God, will answer.
> *Psalm 38:16*

Adoration

Lord God, we come to adore you.
You are the ground of all that is.
You hold us in being, and without you we
    could not be.
Before we were born, before time began,
before the universe came into being, you were;
When time is finished, when the universe is no
    more.
you will still be.
Nothing can take your power from you.
And in your presence we can only be silent
before the mystery of your being, for no words
    of ours can do justice to your glory.

(silence)

O Supreme Lord of the Universe,
you fill and sustain everything around us:
With the touch of your hand you turned
chaos into order, darkness into light.
Unknown energies you hid in the heart of
    matter.
From you bursts forth the splendour of the
    sun,
and the mild radiance of the moon.
Stars and planets without number you set in
    ordered movement.
You are the source of the fire's heat and the
    wind's might,
of the water's coolness and the earth's
    stability.
Deep and wonderful are the mysteries of your
    creation.

157

We adore you, you are beyond all form!
You give form to everything. Lord of all
    creation.

God of all salvation,
you formed us in your own image.
You created us male and female,
you willed our union and harmony.
You entrusted the earth to our care
and promised your blessing to all our
    descendants.
You gave us the spirit of discernment to know
    you,
the power of speech to celebrate your glory,
the strength of love to give ourselves in joy to
    you.
In this wondrous way, O God,
you called us to share
in your own being,
your own knowledge,
your own bliss.

In the oneness of the Supreme Spirit,
through Christ who unites all things in his
    fullness
we and the whole creation give to you
honour and glory, thanks and praise,
worship and adoration,
now and in every age, for ever and ever.
    Amen.

World Council of Churches

Praise

All-Highest, Almighty; our good Lord;

All praise is thine, and glory and honour, and all blessing.

To thee alone, the All-Highest, are they befitting; no man being worthy so much as to name thee.

Praised be thou, my Lord, with all thy creatures – above all our noble brother sun who gives us the day; through him thy light does shine upon us; he tells us of thee, the All-Highest.

Praised be thou, my Lord, through sister moon and the stars. Thou hast set them as heavenly lights, precious and lovely.

Praised be thou, my Lord, through the wind, our brother, and through the air and the clouds and clear sky, and every kind of weather – through which thou yieldest life to all thy creatures.

Praised be thou, my Lord, through our sister water, who serves us in all humility; she is so precious and so pure.

Praised be thou, my Lord, through our brother fire through whom thou dost adorn the night. He is beautiful and joyous, valiant and mighty.

Praised be thou, my Lord, through our sister mother-earth. She sustains us all; but her laws we must obey. She yields all variety of fruits and flowers with all their colours, and the grass of the field.

Praised be thou, my Lord, through those who out of thy love do forgive, those who endure weakness and tribulation. 'Blessed are the peacemakers': from thee, on high, they shall receive the 'crown of life'.

Praised be thou, my Lord, for our sister bodily death, whom no man living can escape. Alas for those who die in mortal sin. Blessed are they who shall be found at one with thy most sacred will – they 'shall not be hurt of the second death'.

Praise and bless my Lord; thank him always, and serve him with utter humility.

St Francis of Assisi, Laudes Creaturarum

The blowing wind,
the mild, moist air,
the exquisite greening
of trees and grasses –

In their beginning,
in their ending,
they give God their praise.

Hildegard of Bingen

Thanksgiving

I cannot dance, O Lord,
unless you lead me.
    If you will
that I leap joyfully
then you must be the first to dance
    and to sing!

Then, and only then,
will I leap for joy.

Then will I soar
    from love to knowledge,
    from knowledge to fruition,
    from fruition to beyond
    all human sense.
And there
    I will remain
    and circle for evermore.
                    Mechtild of Magdeburg

Read Psalm 66

ENDING

Too late came I to love thee, O thou Beauty both so ancient and so fresh, yea too late came I to love thee. And behold, thou wert within me, and I out of myself, where I made search for thee: I ugly rushed headlong upon those beautiful things thou hast made. Thou indeed wert with me; but I was not with thee: these beauties kept me far enough from thee: even those, which unless they were in thee, would not be at all. Thou calledst and criedst unto me, yea thou even breakedst open my deafness: thou discoveredst thy beams and shinedst unto me, and didst cast away my blindness: thou didst most fragrantly blow upon me, and I drew in my breath and I panted after thee; I tasted thee, and now do hunger and thirst after thee; thou didst touch me, and I ever burn again to enjoy thy peace. *St Augustine*

Meditation

My God,
I pray that I may so know you and love you
that I may rejoice in you.
And if I may not do so fully in this life,
let me go steadily on
to the day when I come to that fullness.
Let the knowledge of you increase in me here,
and there let it come to its fullness.
Let your love grow in me here,
and there let it be fulfilled,
so that here my joy may be in a great hope,
and there in full reality.

Lord,
you have commanded, or rather advised us,
to ask by your Son,
and you have promised that we shall receive,
'that our joy may be full'.
That which you counsel
through our 'wonderful counsellor'
is what I am asking for, Lord.
Let me receive
that which you promised through your truth,
'that my joy may be full'.

God of truth,
I ask that I may receive,
so that my joy may be full.
Meanwhile, let my mind meditate on it,
    let my tongue speak of it,
    let my heart love it,
    let my mouth preach it,
    let my soul hunger for it,
    my flesh thirst for it,
    and my whole being desire it,

until I enter into the joy of my Lord,
who is God one and triune, blessed forever.
  Amen.

St Anselm[49]

Here down my wearied limbs I'll lay;
My pilgrim's staff; my weed of grey:
My palmer's hat; my scallop shell;
My cross; my cord; and all farewell.
Robert Herrick (1591–1674)

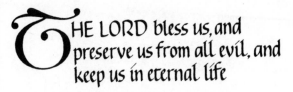

THE LORD bless us, and preserve us from all evil, and keep us in eternal life

THE DAILY OFFICE

BLESSINGS

Do thou, O God, bless unto me
Each thing mine eye doth see;
Do thou, O God, bless unto me
Each sound that comes to me;
Do thou, O God, bless unto me
Each savour that I smell;
Do thou, O God, bless unto me
Each taste in mouth doth dwell;
Each sound that goes unto my song,
Each ray that guides my way,
Each thing that I pursue along,
Each lure that tempts to stray,
The Zeal that seeks my living soul,
The Three that seek my heart and whole,
The Zeal that seeks my living soul,
The Three that seek my heart and whole.

Source unknown (Early Scottish)

May the love of the Father enfold us, the wisdom of the Son enlighten us, the fire of the Spirit inflame us; and may the blessing of the triune God rest upon us, and abide with us, now and evermore.   *Source unknown*

May the peace of the Lord Christ go with you,
    wherever He may send you,
may He guide you through the wilderness,
    protect you through the storm.
May He bring you home rejoicing
    at the wonders He has shown you,

may He bring you home rejoicing
    once again into our doors.

Celtic Daily Prayer

May God shield you on every steep,
May Christ keep you in every path,
May Spirit bathe you in every pass.

Carmina Gadelica III 20

Deep peace of the running wave to you,
Deep peace of the flowing air to you,
Deep peace of the quiet earth to you,
Deep peace of the shining stars to you,
Deep peace of the Son of Peace to you,
    for ever.

Source unknown (Early Scottish)

May the everlasting Father Himself take
    you
In His own generous clasp,
In His own generous arm.

Carmina Gadelica III 201

May God's blessing be yours,
And well may it befall you.

Carmina Gadelica III 205

May God the Father bless us;
May Christ take care of us;
The Holy Spirit enlighten us all the days
    of our life.
The Lord be our Defender and Keeper of
    body and soul,
both now and for ever, to the ages of
    ages.

The Book of Cerne (tenth century)

May the God of hope fill you with all joy and peace as you trust in him, so that you may over-flow with hope by the power of the Holy Spirit.

Romans 15:13 N.I.V.

See that ye be at peace among
　　yourselves, my children,
And love one another.
Follow the example of good men of old
And God will comfort you and help you,
Both in this world
And in the world which is to come.

Celtic Daily Prayer

May the love of the Lord Jesus draw you
　　to himself:
May the power of the Lord Jesus
　　strengthen you in his service.
May the joy of the Lord Jesus fill your
　　spirit
And the Blessing of God Almighty, the
　　Father, the Son and the
Holy Spirit, be upon you and remain with
　　you forever. Amen.

The guarding of the God of life be on you,
The guarding of loving Christ be on you,
The guarding of Holy Spirit be on you
Every night of your lives,
To aid you and enfold you
Each day and night of your lives.

Carmina Gadelica III 207

The love and affection of the angels be to you,
The love and affection of the saints be to you,
The love and affection of heaven be to you,
To guard you and to cherish you.

Carmina Gadelica III 207

May God the Father bless us; may Christ take
care of us; the Holy Ghost enlighten us all the
days of our life. The Lord be our defender and
keeper of body and soul, both now and for ever,
to the ages of ages. *Æthelwold c. 908 – 84*

May the road rise to meet you,
May the wind be always at your back,
May the sun shine warm upon your face,
May the rains fall softly upon your fields.
Until we meet again,
May God hold you in the hollow of His hand.

Source unknown (Celtic)

Lead us from death to life,
    from falsehood to truth.
Lead us from dispair to hope,
    from fear to trust.
Lead us from hate to love,
    from war to peace.
Let peace fill our heart, our world, our universe.

Go in peace: the wisdom of the Wonderful Coun-
sellor guide you, the strength of the Mighty
God defend you, the love of the Everlasting
Father enfold you, the peace of the Prince of
Peace be upon you. And the blessing of God
Almighty, Father, Son, and Holy Spirit be upon
you all this night and for evermore.

Source unknown

May the Lord bless you and protect you.
May the Lord smile on you and show you His
favour.
May the Lord befriend you and prosper you.

Source unknown

May God shield you on every steep,
May Christ aid you on every path,
May Spirit fill you on every slope,
On hill and on plain.

Carmina Gadelica III 209

May God make safe to you each steep,
May God make open to you each pass,
May God make clear to you each road,
And may He take you in the clasp of His
own two hands.

Carmina Gadelica III 203

May the God of peace make you perfect and
holy; and may you be kept safe and blameless,
spirit, soul and body, for the coming of our
Lord Jesus Christ. God has called you and he
will not fail you. *1 Thessalonians 5: 23–24* J.B.

May grace and eternal life be with all who love
our Lord Jesus Christ. *Ephesians 6: 24* J.B.

I lie down this night with God,
And God will lie down with me;
I lie down this night with Christ,
And Christ will lie down with me;
I lie down this night with the Spirit,
And the Spirit will lie down with me;
God and Christ and the Spirit
Be lying down with me.

Carmina Gadelica III 333

May the everlasting Father shield you
East and West wherever you go.

Carmina Gadelica III 202

May Christ's safe-guard protect you ever.

Carmina Gadelica III 203

May God give us light to guide us,
courage to support us,
and love to unit us,
now and evermore.

Source unknown

May the grace of the Lord Jesus sanctify us and
keep us from all evil; may He drive from us all
hurtful things, and purify both our souls and
bodies; may He bind us to Himself by the bond
of love, and may His peace abound in our
hearts.   *Gregorian Sacramentary (sixth century)*

The Lord bless us, and preserve us from all evil,
and keep us in eternal life.   *The Daily Office*

ACKNOWLEDGMENTS

1 Taken from Psalm 51 in the *Grail Psalms*, inclusive language edition, HarperCollins, 1993

2 A Baptismal Creed from *An Alternative Order for Morning and Evening Prayer*, © The Representative Body of the Church in Wales, 1992

3 Adapted from Brendan O'Malley, *A Welsh Pilgrim's Manual*, Gomer Press, Llandysul, Dyfed, 1989 (second ed. 1995)

4 Ibid.

5 Poems of Sir Walter Raleigh taken from *In love with Love – 100 of the greatest mystical poems*, Anne and Christopher Freemantle, eds, Spiritual Masters Series, Paulist Press, NY, 1978

6 'Stopping by Woods on a Snowy Evening' from Robert Frost, *Selected Poems,* Jonathan Cape Ltd, 1980

7 *Carmina Gadelica,* a collection of poems and songs by Alexander Carmichael, Scottish Academic Press, Edinburgh 1976

8 *Homage to Ann Griffiths*, © The Representative Body of the Church in Wales, Church in Wales Publications, 1976.

9 Collect from *A New Zealand Prayer Book,* The Church of the Province of New Zealand, Collins, 1989

10 Gerard Manley Hopkins, *Poems and Prose,* Penguin, 1963

11 Pierre Teilhard de Chardin, *Hymn of the Universe,* Collins, Fountain Books, 1977

12 St Adamnan's sentence is from Helen Waddell, trans., *The Life of St Columba* (written about 690)

13 'May-time' from *A Celtic Miscellany,* Penguin, 1971

14 'Brother Lizard' from Brian Brendan O'Malley, *The Animals of St. Gregory,* Paulinus Press, 1981

15 Helen Colebrook, 'A Walk on the Moor', from *Earthsong* – a green anthology of poetry, readings and prayers, Churchman Publishing Ltd, 1990

16 As above (*Earthsong*)

17 *Meditations with Hildegard of Bingen,* translated by Gabriele Uhlein, Bear & Co., Inc., 1983

18 From Brian Brendan O'Malley, *A Pilgrim's Manual, St. David's,* Paulinus Press, 1985. For a more extended rite see this manual.

19 From James Carney, *Medieval Irish Lyrics,* Dolmien Press 1985

20 *Meditations with Mechtild of Magdeburg,* translated by Sue Woodruff, Bear & Co. Inc., Santa Fe, N. Mex., 1982

21 Psalm 42 from *Grail Psalms,* inclusive language edition

22 From *Medieval Irish Lyrics*

23 Ibid.

24 From *Medieval Latin Lyrics,* translated by Helen Waddell, Constable, 1930

25 Ibid.

26 Ibid.

27 From *Celtic Christian Spirituality,* edited by

Oliver Davies and Fiona Bowie, SPCK, 1995
and printed with their kind permission

28 From *A Celtic Miscellany*
29 From *More Latin Lyrics,* translated by Helen
    Waddell, Victor Gollancz Ltd, 1976
30 Ibid.
31 From *Medieval Latin Lyrics*
32 From *More Latin Lyrics*
33 Ibid.
34 Ibid.
35 From *Listen to Love* (reflections on the
    seasons of the year), edited by Louis M.
    Savary sj, Geoffrey Chapman, 1970
36 Ibid.
37 From *New English Hymnal,* Canterbury
    Press Norwich
38 From *More Latin Lyrics*
39 From *New English Hymnal*
40 From *Listen to Love*
41 From *Medieval Latin Lyrics*
42 From *New English Hymnal*
43 From *Affirmations and Prayers,* J. Donald
    Walters Crystal Clarity Publishers, Nevada
    City, Calif., 1988
44 St Augustine, 'On Psalm 99', *Drinking from
    the Hidden Fountain,* edited by Thomas Spi-
    dlik, New City, London, 1992, and is printed
    with permission.
45 From *The Oxford Book of Prayer,* Oxford
    University Press, 1985
46 MS of Monte Cassino, from *Medieval Latin
    Lyrics*
47 Patrick Leigh Fermor, *A Time to Keep Silent*,
    John Murray (Publishers) Ltd, 1988.

48 From *The Art of Prayer – an Orthodix Anthology,* Faber, 1966
49 St Anselm, 'Proslogion', from *The Prayers & Meditations of St. Anselm,* translated by Benedicta Ward, Penguin, 1973